A BARTHOLOMEW MAP

WALK THE THAMES & CHILTERNS

BY JILL BROWN AND DAVID SKELHON

JOHN BARTHOLOMEW & SON LTD
EDINBURGH

British Library Cataloguing in Publication Data
Brown, Jill
    Walk the Thames and Chilterns.
    1. Chiltern Hill (England) — Description
    and travel — Guide books 2. Thames,
    River, Valley (England) — Description
    and travel — Guide books
    I. Title II. Skelhon, David
    914.22′04858   DA670.C6

    ISBN 0-7028-0802-4

Published and Printed in Scotland
by John Bartholomew & Son Ltd.,
Duncan Street, Edinburgh EH9 1TA

First edition 1988

Copyright © John Bartholomew & Son Ltd. 1988

Produced for John Bartholomew & Son Ltd
by Curtis Garratt Limited, The Old Vicarage,
Horton cum Studley, Oxford OX9 1BT

Typesetting and maps by Taurus Graphics

Layouts by Burman Associates

ISBN 0 7028 0802 4

The physical landscape of Britain is changing all the time
e.g. as new tracks are made, hedges grubbed up and fields
amalgamated. While every care has been taken in the
preparation of this guide, neither Curtis Garratt Limited nor
John Bartholomew & Son Ltd will be responsible for any loss,
damage or inconvenience caused by inaccuracies.

CONTENTS

KEY MAP FOR THE WALKS

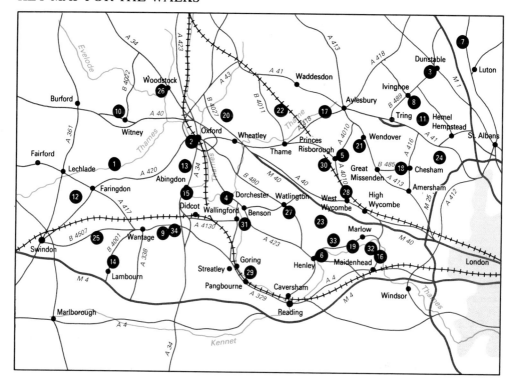

KEY TO SCALE AND MAP SYMBOLS

SCALE 1 : 63 360

SCALE 1 : 25 000

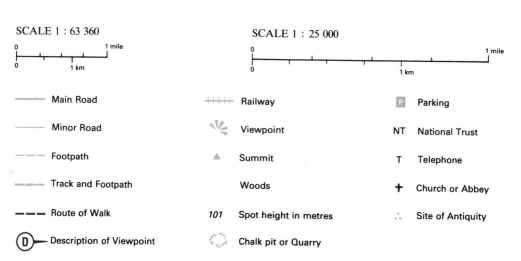

	Main Road	+++++	Railway	P	Parking
	Minor Road	※	Viewpoint	NT	National Trust
	Footpath	▲	Summit	T	Telephone
	Track and Footpath		Woods	+	Church or Abbey
	Route of Walk	*101*	Spot height in metres	∴	Site of Antiquity
Ⓓ	Description of Viewpoint		Chalk pit or Quarry		

4

1 WHY WALK?

At no other time has there been a greater need for easy access to the countryside, especially for those bound one way or another to the urban scene. Rural Britain has so much to offer – much more than just the space for the fresh air and exercise required to counteract increasingly sedentary lifestyles. A walk in the countryside, however brief, brings benefits that transcend such a seemingly humble pursuit.

The pace of modern living makes us slaves to the clock while our technology saturates us with what is often inconsequential information. All this can anaesthetize an already weary mind to anything beyond the necessities of daily life.

By walking, we can break the routine and regain a sense of perspective – the British landscape is rich in history and it can be a humbling but reassuring experience to realize that the track beneath your feet and the view before your eyes have been used and enjoyed by many preceeding generations, no doubt with similar problems and aspirations to our own.

It is, of course, up to the individual to gain full benefit from these rural forays, for the countryside's panacea is there for all who are willing to surrender their minds and senses for the brief hours of their visit. It is also well to remember that a walk should be a series of experiences to be savoured at leisure.

A guidebook such as this can be no more than its name implies – a selective guide to the finest and best that an area has to offer. The hope is that it will encourage further exploration and lead to a greater appreciation of our considerable environmental heritage.

2 CLOTHING AND EQUIPMENT

One of the most important factors in the enjoyment of a walk will be the choice of footwear. Inadequate or ill-fitting boots will cause considerable discomfort and spoil even the most interesting walk.

Lightweight leather boots with good tread to grip on slippery clay slopes are ideal for the Thames and Chilterns. For shorter walks on wet or muddy ground the underrated wellington can be particularly useful.

Waterproof jackets and trousers are imporant, not only for protection from showers but also for warmth on windswept ridges and heights. Over-trousers are also useful when walking through wet crops and tall vegetation which would otherwise leave you soaked from the waist down. In the colder months a hat, such as a balaclava, will conserve a lot of warmth because up to a-third of body heat is lost through an uncovered head.

Although the Thames and Chilterns is not wild, open country, it is important to carry a compass, preferably one of the 'Silva' type, and, of course, the relevant map. Binoculars are not essential but are very useful for spotting distant stiles and give added interest to viewpoints and wildlife. A pair of 8x30s are sufficiently powerful but still light enough to be carried comfortably.

Finally, these items can best be stored in a lightweight rucksack. Nothing too large or heavy is required for day walking and, for comfort, choose a design with wide, padded shoulderstraps.

3 PUBLIC RIGHTS OF WAY

In England and Wales rights of way fall into three main categories:
(a) Public Footpaths – for walkers only
(b) Public Bridleways – for passage on foot, horse-back, or bicycle
(c) Byways – for walkers, cyclists, horse riders, and motorized vehicles.

There is another category: Roads used as Public Paths, such as the Ridgeway, on which horses, bicycles, and motor vehicles may or may not be permitted. These will all eventually be reclassified as one of the three above. Although it may often be impractical, pushchairs, prams, wheelchairs, and invalid carriages may also be taken on to any right of way.

The Highway Authorities are usually responsible for the maintenance of rights of way in their area, and are able to take action against landowners when paths have been unlawfully obstructed, or when misleading signs have been used to discourage the use of a right of way. They are also responsible for the upkeep of the definitive maps which show rights of way – a right of way exists so long as it is on the definitive map. Walkers wishing to consult these maps will find them at the county or district council offices. Copies are also sometimes kept by parish councils or at public libraries.

A walker may linger to admire the view or eat lunch but must not obstruct a right of way. It is up to the walker to ensure that he or she keeps to the designated path for, if he/she wanders away from the public path – either deliberately or unintentional-ly – he/she may be trespassing. This is usually a civil rather than a criminal matter, but the landowner is entitled to sue. The trespassing walker must leave the land immediately if asked to do so by the landowner.

Sooner or later a walker is likely to come across a path blocked by an obstruction. You have the right to remove it just enough to pass by but you cannot go on to a right of way with prior knowledge of an obstruction and the intention to remove it. Growing crops are the most common obstruction. You are entitled to walk through them even if this means some damage is unavoidable. Often this is unpleasant and, with some mature crops, virtually impossible. You may in these circumstances go around the crop, but it is advisable to stay within the field boundary to avoid trespass on someone else's land.

A farmer can plough up a public footpath but must usually reinstate it within two weeks. He is not normally permitted to plough up a footpath which runs along the edge of the field.

The presence of a bull alongside a footpath can be unnerving but not necessarily illegal, for a farmer may turn out a mature beef bull as long as there are cows present. Dairy bulls, the most common being the black-and-white Friesian, are illegal, and the walker should be extremely wary if he sees one although, in practice, it may be difficult for the untrained eye to determine between beef and dairy breeds.

Dogs are allowed on public rights of way if they are under close control. You are liable to prosecution and the dog may be shot if it is found worrying farm animals.

4 THE COUNTRY CODE

The country code can be summed up with the well-known adage 'leave only footprints, take only photographs'. All it takes is a little care and thought. Don't, for instance, drop litter – fluorescent orange peel, crushed drink cans, and brightly coloured chocolate wrappers do not blend well with the environment. Shut all gates and use the proper stiles to cross walls and hedges. On narrow paths walk in single file to avoid unnecessary erosion.

Do not disturb the wildlife and remember that the Wildlife and Countryside Act of 1981 gives strong protection to many wild creatures. Many plants have special protection and must not be picked intentionally. In any case, flowers are there for all to enjoy.

The country code is based on common sense. You will offend no-one if you leave the countryside as you found it.

5 MAP READING

Maps convey a considerable amount of information to the experienced eye, and navigational skills should be acquired by all who wander through the landscape. They are easily learnt but, like all techniques, require practice.

The most useful scale of map for the walker is the 1:25 000 or about 2½ inches to the mile. Features are shown in greater detail than on the 1:50 000 and all public rights of way are easily identifiable in green ink. Most of all, they show field boundaries, which are very useful in determining the route of a path.

Failure to identify your current position correctly is often the first step in becoming lost. To confirm your position, orientate the map with the compass so that the grid of the map lies in line with the needle, which should point to the top of the map. Recognizable landmarks should then relate to those on the map and other features will fit into place. This method is useful but note that it is not quite accurate because the needle points to magnetic north, which currently lies some 6 degrees west of grid north.

Remember that it is easy to make mistakes, and maps do become out of date – hedges are grubbed up, footpaths are diverted. Do not become too carried away with the scenery or overestimate your navigational ability, and make frequent checks on your position.

6 THE THAMES AND CHILTERNS

The Thames and Chilterns is not a dramatic landscape on the scale of Wales or the Lake District but does possess considerable scenic variety. The lush pastoral scenery of the clay lowlands contrasts sharply with the higher, drier chalk country while the chalk itself changes in character from the open, short-turfed downs in Berkshire to the wooded and more populous Chilterns.

It is an interesting exercise, when travelling around an area, to note the regional differences and the interplay between human and natural features. The countryside reflects the nature of its physical foundations and such surface features as vegetation, settlement siting, farming practices, and building materials are influenced by, and reminders of, the underlying rock.

Geology
The general geological pattern is one of alternating vales and scarps oriented north-east to south-west, with the oldest rocks in the north-west. The area lies between the Cotswold limestone belt in the north-west and the chalk to the south-east, with a lowland vale between composed of clays and split into two by a thin line of Corallian limestone hills. To the north of these hills lies a vale of Oxford Clay drained by the Thames, and to the south a vale of Kimmeridge and Gault Clay drained by the Ock and the Thame.

In its upper reaches, the Thames flows along the Oxford Clay before turning south-east to cut through the Corallian ridge at Oxford. It then flows south through the Kimmeridge/Gault vale towards the chalk, where it has cut a gap that is commonly, if not quite accurately, held to be the dividing line between the Downs and the Chilterns.

The rocks were deposited and subjected to cycles of erosion and uplift under conditions that bore no resemblance to the modern scene. During the Jurassic period, beginning 190 million years ago, most of England and Wales was invaded by the sea and received deposits of limestone and mud that we now know as the Cotswolds and the Oxford/Kimmeridge Clay. Conditions changed and the clearer water encouraged the appearance of corals so that the Oxford area at this time was a tropical sea dotted with coral reefs. Today, these form the heights around Oxford and the pronounced scarp to Faringdon.

These rocks were uplifted to the south and east and submerged by the sea once again during the Cretaceous period, 120 million years ago. Rivers brought sediments of sand and mud that later consolidated into the Greensand and Gault Clay while, later still, the bodies of innumerable minute marine creatures accumulated on the sea floor to form chalk rock thousands of feet thick.

Another period of uplift ended the deposition, and the rocks were once again tilted to the south and east, and subjected to erosion by wind and rain. Rainwater containing carbonic acid dissolved the chalk as well as the silica from the skeletons of sponges also within the rock and redeposited the latter as flint in the upper layers of the chalk. The magnificent Chiltern woodlands are supported by this clay-with-flints mixed with remnants of a sandy layer later deposited during the Eocene period, around 64 million years ago.

The last major period of uplift occurred about 30 million years ago during the activity of the Alpine movement. It raised the chalk into comparative mountains so that the subdued countryside we see today is but the worn-down remnants.

Features of the chalk country

Chalk is not a homogeneous rock and contains layers of varying hardnesses that have led to 'steps' in the scarp slope. Geologists divide the rock into Lower, Middle, and Upper, the latter being very white and containing the flints. On large parts of the Downs, the Upper Chalk has been eroded away and is covered by chalk-tolerant turf but, on the Chilterns, the presence of the Upper Chalk and its clay-with-flints supports ponds and woodland.

Along the foot of the escarpment is a pronounced terrace. In the west, a fertile bench of Greensand supports a string of settlements including Wantage and Wallingford while, further east, a bench of

Lower Chalk underlies villages that have been attracted by the proximity of water and easier communications.

Because surface water is scarce on the porous chalk, the presence of dry valleys – or coombes – is surprising. They were possibly cut either when the water table was much higher than at present or during the Ice Ages, when the frozen subsoil acted as an impermeable layer.

The isolated blocks of rock seen in chalk country are known as sarsens. They originate from the sandy Eocene beds which were cemented into hard sandstone by silica-laden groundwater and, on exposure, weathered into the blocks seen today. Like flint, which was highly valued for its hardness and sharpness, sarsens were of great significance to Neolithic people who used them in the construction of megaliths.

The Ridgeway

Although the officially designated path is only 85 miles (137 km) long, this ancient track traverses the Thames and Chilterns on a route that once stretched from the Dorset coast to the Wash. It can be considered the oldest road in Europe, most probably walked even before the onset of the last Ice Age. It offered a high route clear of the dangers and difficulties of the densely wooded lowland, and was used by a succession of early immigrants as a route to inland Britain. The Romans, on the other hand, largely ignored its potential for troop movement because of its distance from water supplies. In the eighteenth century, however, it became popular once again with sheep and cattle drovers who wished to avoid the turnpike tolls on the way to markets in London.

East of the Thames, the path is known as the Icknield Way – a younger, but still ancient, route. In many places, this path is a surfaced road but it splits into Upper and Lower paths. The Upper follows the foot of the escarpment but the Lower gave access to settlement and water. The presence of two parallel routes appears odd but it is possible that they were used according to the seasons and the weather.

The Thames

The Thames is 215 miles (346 km) long and the longest river wholly in England, but the Severn exceeds it by 5 miles (8 km). It has played an influential historical role and, from early times, held considerable economic and strategic importance. It formed part of the boundary between Wessex and Mercia and delimited the southern extent of the Danelaw. During the Civil War, there were fierce skirmishes for control of key bridges and, later still, it was incorporated into modern county boundaries.

As a trade artery, it was important as early as Saxon times. In the Middle Ages, the main cargo was wool; in Tudor times, it was coal and food, mostly transported by barge. By the early nineteenth century, the river was linked to the central canal network and only decreased in importance after the coming of the railways.

Although today it is a highly organized river, navigation until the end of the eighteenth century was a laborious affair largely due to the proliferation of flash weirs for mills and fisheries. These made navigation slow and expensive and greatly reduced general fish stocks. There was a clause in *Magna Carta* ordering all weirs to be removed but this was ignored. The situation worsened and, in 1605, James I appointed eighteen Commissioners to improve the river at a particularly bad spot between Oxford and Burcot. The outcome was the construction of the first pound locks on the Thames in the 1630s. This design was introduced along the rest of the river and today boats drawing 3 feet (90 cm) can reach as far as Lechlade.

The river changes noticeably in character along its length. The lower section, near to large centres of population, is comparatively busy with river traffic and walkers. The central section presents grander scenery with beautiful tree-clad banks, and the upper reaches become increasingly more peaceful and remote. Downstream of Oxford, the Thames is flanked by bustling riverside communities, in contrast to the river above Godstow to Lechlade where the meadows are largely devoid of human habitation.

Here the villages stand back from the river on their gravel terraces above the floodplain.

Those exploring this countryside for the first time may be surprised by the abundance of quiet backwaters and the richness of the historical legacy. This is a subtle landscape but probably contains enough variety to suit the taste of most walkers.

7 PLANTS AND ANIMALS

The Thames and Chilterns is an interesting area for the natural historian because there is a variety of habitats, each supporting its own plants and animals.

A walk on the chalk during the growing season is likely to be a colourful affair. Of the many typical flowers, the most seen include the pea family, wild thyme, wild basil and marjoram, rockroses, cowslips, mulleins, violets, gentians, eyebright, and harebells. Of the orchids, the two most frequently encountered are the pyramid and fragrant orchids.

Flitting between these is a variety of beautiful butterflies, including several of Britain's native blue species. Also look out for the orange-tip, the brimstone, and the attractive marbled white. Some birds of the downland are the corn bunting, wheatears, and whinchats, and the walker may well be accompanied by the song of the lark and meadow pipit or the call of the lapwing.

Spring in the Chiltern woodland is likely to mean a profusion of bluebells. The clay-with-flints will later support bugle, yellow archangel, sweet woodruff, herb Robert, and enchanter's nightshade. Among the trees are nuthatches, treecreepers, and woodpeckers.

On the damper lowlands, the ditches and rivers are lined with willow, alder, and reedmace. The water supports arrowhead and pondweeds and, on the banks, there may be the delightful ragged robin. Water-loving birds are numerous – mute swans, moorhens, and herons while, on the gravel pits and reservoirs, there are Canada geese and various species of duck.

RUSHEY LOCK

0   1 mile

0   1 km

4¾ miles (7½ km) Easy; sections by the Thames may be overgrown

The upper Thames to Lechlade lacks riverside villages of any size and can seem a world away from the bustle of the lower river. This stretch is free from the sight and sound of road traffic and, after Rushey Lock, empty of human habitation.

The first lock was constructed in 1790 but was rebuilt in 1898. It is the weir, however, that holds most interest because it is one of very few paddle weirs left on the river. Paddle and rymer weirs were used for centuries – in medieval times, they were con

structed of stakes and brushwood. They were laborious to operate, however, and not a little hazardous for the boats. They were gradually replaced by pound locks and mechanically operated sluices but existed well into this century. The last one remained until 1937.

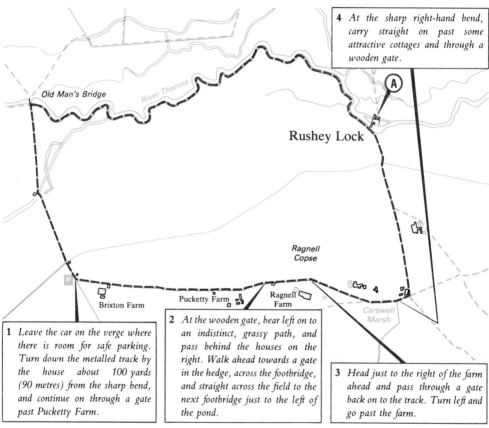

4 *At the sharp right-hand bend, carry straight on past some attractive cottages and through a wooden gate.*

Old Man's Bridge

River Thames

Rushey Lock

Ⓐ

Ragnell Copse

Brixton Farm

Pucketty Farm

Ragnell Farm

Carswell Marsh

1 *Leave the car on the verge where there is room for safe parking. Turn down the metalled track by the house about 100 yards (90 metres) from the sharp bend, and continue on through a gate past Pucketty Farm.*

2 *At the wooden gate, bear left on to an indistinct, grassy path, and pass behind the houses on the right. Walk ahead towards a gate in the hedge, across the footbridge, and straight across the field to the next footbridge just to the left of the pond.*

3 *Head just to the right of the farm ahead and pass through a gate back on to the track. Turn left and go past the farm.*

A Paddle weirs were constructed of horizontal beams and vertical rymers and paddles. First of all a heavy wooden beam would be laid on the riverbed, often in a masonry sill. A second beam would be placed over this, above the water level, and secured at the sides. This beam was meant to be removable or swung aside. There would be sockets at intervals on the lower beam into which were

Over

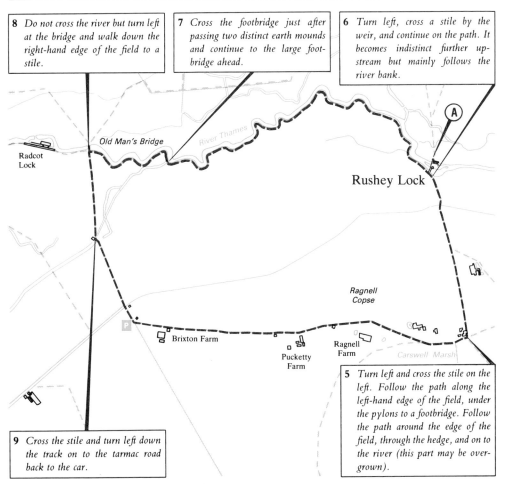

8 *Do not cross the river but turn left at the bridge and walk down the right-hand edge of the field to a stile.*

7 *Cross the footbridge just after passing two distinct earth mounds and continue to the large footbridge ahead.*

6 *Turn left, cross a stile by the weir, and continue on the path. It becomes indistinct further upstream but mainly follows the river bank.*

Old Man's Bridge

River Thames

Radcot Lock

Rushey Lock

Ragnell Copse

Brixton Farm

Pucketty Farm

Ragnell Farm

Carswell Marsh

5 *Turn left and cross the stile on the left. Follow the path along the left-hand edge of the field, under the pylons to a footbridge. Follow the path around the edge of the field, through the hedge, and on to the river (this part may be overgrown).*

9 *Cross the stile and turn left down the track on to the tarmac road back to the car.*

placed square-sectioned timbers, or rymers, positioned on the upstream side so that the current held them in place. Against the rymers were placed boards on long wooden handles – the 'paddles' – which held up the water.

To open the weir, the keeper would first withdraw the paddles, then the rymers [which can weigh about 100 pounds (45 kg)], and finally the upper beam. Boats would then wait for the first rush of water to subside then 'flash' through if going downstream or be hauled by winch, men, or horses if going upstream.

Traffic now uses the easier, if less spectacular, modern locks, but the remaining paddle weirs are still used in controlling the river level.

OXFORD AND GODSTOW LOCK

5¾ miles (9¼ km) Easy

0   1 mile
0   1 km

This is largely a waterside walk, with a wide range of history and scenery. Lewis Carroll is reputed to have gained inspiration for *Alice in Wonderland* while rowing Alice Liddell along this stretch of the Thames in 1862.

2 *Go through the gate and on to the next bridge ahead. Cross the river and turn right, following the path past Godstow Lock to the road.*

3 *Turn right through Wolvercote and continue as far as the railway bridge.*

4 *Walk on the left-hand side over the bridge, then turn left down-slope (this is slippery when wet) on to the towpath by Wolvercote Lock. Turn right and continue beside the canal.*

Wytham Great Wood

Wytham

Wolvercote

Godstow Abbey (remains of)

Godstow Lock

B

River Thames

A

Round Hill

A 34(T)

A 420

Oxford Canal

River Cherwell

C

Oxford

P

Botley

1 *It is usually possible to park in Abbey or Cripley Roads off the main Botley Road (A420) next to the railway station. However, there is a three-hour limit here and parking may be easier in the city car parks or on side roads further from the centre. Alternatively, the walk may begin from the car park about ¼ mile (400 m) east of The Trout Inn in Lower Wolvercote. Starting in Oxford, walk to the end of Abbey Road and turn left down a path to a footbridge. Cross this and turn left along the Thames.*

6 *Turn left over the footbridge ahead, then left back to the end of Abbey Road.*

5 *At Isis Lock, branch off to the right of Bridge 243 and over another bridge. Cross over the old siding, past a disused railway swingbridge, and then underneath the railway.*

A Port Meadow has been grazed and cut for hay since the Bronze Age but, for the last 1000 years, it has been the property of the Freemen of the City of Oxford. Never ploughed or sprayed with chemicals, it is of considerable ecological importance. When frozen after winter floods, it becomes an outdoor skating rink.

B Godstow Nunnery was once a fine complex of buildings but the Dissolution and Civil War reduced it to ruins. It was founded in 1133 for Benedictine nuns but its most notable inhabitant was Fair Rosamund – mistress of Henry II.

C When completed in 1790, the Oxford-to-Coventry Canal formed a direct link from the Thames to the Midland coalfield. The main cargo was coal, carried by barges still mainly horse drawn to the middle of this century. Trade declined with competition from the railways and finally ceased in the early 1960s.

12

Walk 3

TOTTERNHOE KNOLLS

3¾ miles (6 km) Moderate; very muddy in parts

There are good views on this walk over to Dunstable Downs, where gliders may be seen riding the thermals above the ridge. The area has long been quarried, and many fine buildings have used Totternhoe 'clunch' stone in their construction, including Hampton Court and Windsor Castle.

> **5** *Turn left up a rough road, which soon becomes a dirt track, and follow it uphill. Cross the second stile on the right about 75 yards (70 metres) before the sharp right-hand bend and cross the nature reserve, heading uphill for a stile in the far left-hand corner.*

> **4** *Turn left and go straight on when the track becomes a tarmac road. At the T-junction, turn left for 150 yards (135 metres).*

> **3** *Turn left along the track, passing close to Maiden Bower on the left which can be glimpsed through the hedge. Continue along the track as far as the limeworks, crossing over the first track to a second just beyond, and then turning right to a T-junction.*

Dismantled Railway — Sewell Farm — Sewell — Chalk Pit — Maiden Bower — **A** — Pit (dis) — **B** — Lower End — **T** — Motte & Baileys — Castle Hill — 160 — **D** — Middle End — **C** — Dunstable — Totternhoe — **P**

> **6** *Cross the stile and continue ahead on the track, bearing left at the first junction. At the next junction, continue on down the narrow path back to the car park.*

> **1** *Park in the car park signposted from the road through Totternhoe village. At the information board, take the path immediately to the left and turn right at the top of the steps to a junction with a grassy track.*

> **2** *Turn right along the track, from which there are good views across to the Dunstable Downs. Go left at the next junction and then right after 150 yards (135 metres). Follow this track until it crosses another track at the end of the tall hedges.*

A Maiden Bower is a Neolithic causewayed camp dated about 3500 BC and some 700 feet (213 m) in diameter.

B Totternhoe Stone is a harder, grey band in the Lower Chalk, mined here since 200 BC. Competition from the harder Portland Stone last century led to a decline but it is still used for agricultural lime and building.

C This Local Nature Reserve is a Site of Special Scientific Interest (SSSI). Its 34 acres (14 ha) of chalk downland and beechwood harbour many plants and animals that are rare or restricted in distribution.

D The triangulation point stands on the keep of a once-extensive Norman motte and bailey castle, possibly built to protect the quarries in the twelfth century.

Walk 4

Walk 4

WITTENHAM CLUMPS AND DORCHESTER

4¾ miles (7½ km) Moderate; one steep climb

This part of the Thames has a long history of occupation. Here the river receives one of its major tributaries and, at this site, developed a settlement whose later influence was out of all proportion to its size.

Dorchester is one of England's oldest cities and, due to the work of St Birinus, became as important a centre for Christianity as Canterbury. It was first the cathedral city of Wessex, then of Mercia, and the surviving Abbey church is held to be one of the greatest ecclesiastical buildings of south-ern England.

The walk also includes one of the best viewpoints in Oxford-shire – quickly approached at the beginning but not quite so easily gained at the end!

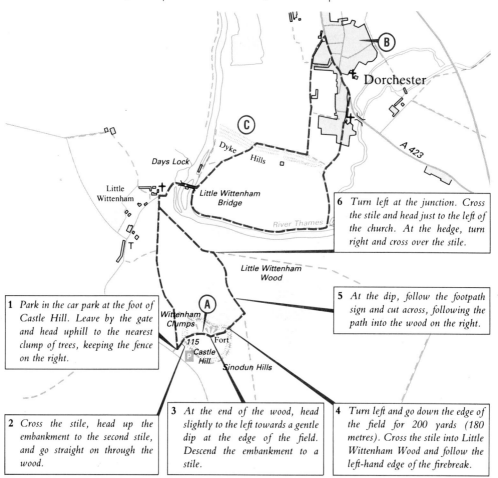

1 *Park in the car park at the foot of Castle Hill. Leave by the gate and head uphill to the nearest clump of trees, keeping the fence on the right.*

2 *Cross the stile, head up the embankment to the second stile, and go straight on through the wood.*

3 *At the end of the wood, head slightly to the left towards a gentle dip at the edge of the field. Descend the embankment to a stile.*

4 *Turn left and go down the edge of the field for 200 yards (180 metres). Cross the stile into Little Wittenham Wood and follow the left-hand edge of the firebreak.*

5 *At the dip, follow the footpath sign and cut across, following the path into the wood on the right.*

6 *Turn left at the junction. Cross the stile and head just to the left of the church. At the hedge, turn right and cross over the stile.*

Over

14

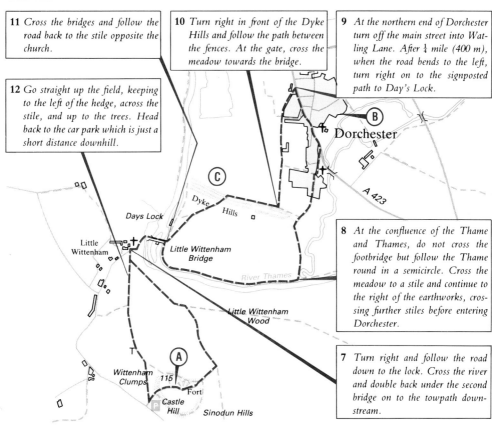

11 *Cross the bridges and follow the road back to the stile opposite the church.*

10 *Turn right in front of the Dyke Hills and follow the path between the fences. At the gate, cross the meadow towards the bridge.*

9 *At the northern end of Dorchester turn off the main street into Watling Lane. After ¼ mile (400 m), when the road bends to the left, turn right on to the signposted path to Day's Lock.*

12 *Go straight up the field, keeping to the left of the hedge, across the stile, and up to the trees. Head back to the car park which is just a short distance downhill.*

8 *At the confluence of the Thame and Thames, do not cross the footbridge but follow the Thame round in a semicircle. Cross the meadow to a stile and continue to the right of the earthworks, crossing further stiles before entering Dorchester.*

7 *Turn right and follow the road down to the lock. Cross the river and double back under the second bridge on to the towpath downstream.*

A This series of prominent hills, composed largely of Upper Greensand and capped with Lower Chalk, gives superb panoramic views over the Thames and its valley, some 200 feet (60 m) below.

Castle Hill was an Iron Age hill fort but was also later fortified in the eighth century.

B The Romans were attracted here by the strategic river crossing on the road from Silchester to Alcester. The Saxons had arrived by the fifth century and in AD 635 received St Birinus, a missionary from Rome. His most important convert was Cynegils, King of Wessex, who was baptized in the Thame nearby.

Dorchester was once the largest diocese in England but the bishopric was transferred to Lincoln in 1072 and the cathedral later became an Augustinian abbey. This was largely destroyed in the Dissolution but the Abbey church was saved by a townsman who bought it for £140!

C The Dyke Hills comprise two massive banks and a ditch – probably filled with water from the Thames – which enclose 115 acres (46 ha). They are thought to be Iron Age.

ASKETT AND WHITELEAF

0   1 mile
0   1 km

$4\frac{1}{2}$ miles (7 km) Moderate; one steep climb

Many elements of the typical Chilterns scene are present here – the escarpment view, beechwood, and downland. In contrast, though, the walk begins in low-lying eadow, passing near to a site of consideable historic importance and through a peaceful Bucking- hamshire village before climbing the hillside.

2 *Follow the left-hand field boundary to the next stile. Cross the track and stile opposite, then angle half-right across the field to the left-hand edge of the trees.*

1 *Park in the lay-by off the A4010 just to the south of Great Kimble church. Cross the road and pass through the kissing gate opposite the northern end of the lay-by. Angle left across some pleasant meadowland to the stile in the far corner by the telegraph pole.*

3 *Turn left and continue along the left-hand edge of the fields.*

4 *Cross to the right of the trees and walk straight ahead. Follow the path around to the road.*

5 *Turn right then first left down Askett Lane. Turn left at the end of the lane.*

6 *Cross the stile and walk ahead for about 100 yards (90 m) to the end of the grassy track; then angle back to the right to a stile just in front of a large red-brick house.*

7 *Cross the stile ahead and continue down the right-hand edge of the field. Cross the marshy area and turn half-left to a footbridge. Follow the footpath off to the left, through the buildings to the road.*

Smoky Row

Great Kimble

Moats

Old Grange

A4010

Askett House

Askett

248 Fort

Pulpit Hill

Lower Cadsden

Whiteleaf

Giles Wood

Whiteleaf Cross

Monks Risborough

A The name of Great Kimble is derived from Cymbeline, a British king of Roman times. The village played a much more recent historical role during the years leading up to the Civil War, however, for it was here, in January 1635, that John Hampden refused to pay his Ship Money tax of 20 shillings. This was one of the first events in the clash between King and Parliament that was to divide the county.

B Standing in the clearing at the top of the hill at 750 feet (228 m), there are good views out over the Aylesbury plain.

Over

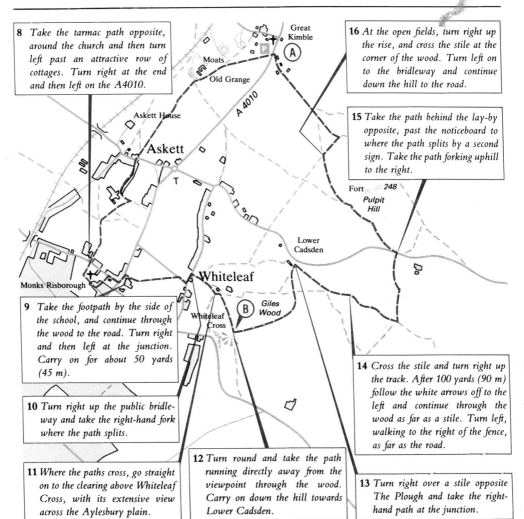

8 Take the tarmac path opposite, around the church and then turn left past an attractive row of cottages. Turn right at the end and then left on the A4010.

16 At the open fields, turn right up the rise, and cross the stile at the corner of the wood. Turn left on to the bridleway and continue down the hill to the road.

15 Take the path behind the lay-by opposite, past the noticeboard to where the path splits by a second sign. Take the path forking uphill to the right.

9 Take the footpath by the side of the school, and continue through the wood to the road. Turn right and then left at the junction. Carry on for about 50 yards (45 m).

14 Cross the stile and turn right up the track. After 100 yards (90 m) follow the white arrows off to the left and continue through the wood as far as a stile. Turn left, walking to the right of the fence, as far as the road.

10 Turn right up the public bridle-way and take the right-hand fork where the path splits.

11 Where the paths cross, go straight on to the clearing above Whiteleaf Cross, with its extensive view across the Aylesbury plain.

12 Turn round and take the path running directly away from the viewpoint through the wood. Carry on down the hill towards Lower Cadsden.

13 Turn right over a stile opposite The Plough and take the right-hand path at the junction.

Whiteleaf Cross cannot be seen at this point but begins a few yards below the summit, stretching down for 80 feet (24 m) and across for 72 feet (22 m). There is no definite opinion on its age and purpose and was for a long time thought to be Anglo Saxon. It is now believed to be much younger, perhaps seventeenth century. A charter of AD 903, however, refers to a boundary marker here so, whatever the age of the present cross, it may be of much older origin.

Walk 6
HAMBLEDEN LOCK AND HENLEY

6 miles (9½ km) Moderate; in early July, the towpath near Henley bridge is closed during the Regatta. Walkers must proceed around the back of the enclosures

Allow more time than usual for this walk to look at the views of the mill and Henley's attractive waterfront. This is a famous stretch of the river, and its tranquil waters provide a fitting end to a relatively undemanding, but rewarding day's walk.

1 *The walk starts from the car park beside the Hambleden road, ¼ mile (400 m) from Mill End. Turn right out of the car park.*

2 *Turn right at the junction and, after 50 yards (45 m), turn left by a wooden fence, following the path round to the front of the mill. Walk across the weirs and lock gates and turn left on the towpath by the river.*

9 *Follow the towpath all the way back to Hambleden Lock and retrace the route back to the car park.*

3 *Leave the towpath at the footpath sign and follow the track round to the right as far as the road. Turn left and then right by the Flower Pot Hotel.*

8 *Just before the bridge, turn right down a driveway, and take the left-hand footpath between the fence and the hedge down to the river. Turn right.*

4 *Turn right just past the last house and follow the hedge. Carry straight on along the dirt track to the road and turn left.*

7 *Aim diagonally to the far corner, cross the stile, and continue to the road. Turn left and then right on the A423.*

6 *Cross the stile at the end of the wood and go straight across the field to the path by the wooden fence. Keep on the path to a grassy field.*

5 *Turn right at the footpath sign and follow the path across the field and through Remenham Wood.*

Map labels: Hambleden, ROMAN VILLA (site of), Mill End, Mill, Hambleden Lock, A, Remenham, Aston, A 423, A 4155, River Thames, Remenham Wood, B, Henley, A 423

A The cluster of weatherboarded mill, house, weirs, and lasher pools seems to slot so naturally into the landscape, and the turbulence of the weir adds an interesting dynamic touch. The Domesday survey recorded a mill hereabouts but the present building is six-teenth century, and was working until 1958.

B Henley's early prosperity centred on the river and bridge. In the eighteenth century, it was an important staging post for the Oxford to London coaches, and later became a fashionable social centre. There are many fine Georgian buildings, and the elegant bridge dates from 1786.

The Regatta was first held in 1839 and now covers a course of 1 mile 550 yards (approximately 2 km), upstream of Temple Island.

SHARPENHOE CLAPPERS

$2\frac{3}{4}$ miles ($4\frac{1}{2}$ km) Easy/Moderate; one steep climb

At the northern tip of the Chilterns, Sharpenhoe Clappers offers good views over the Bedfordshire countryside. It was given to the National Trust in 1939, and its rich assemblage of characteristic chalk plants and animals has earned it the status of a Site of Special Scientific Interest (SSSI).

The short woodland section is delightful in summer when the ground is carpeted with the white and pink flowers of enchanter's nightshade and herb Robert.

4 *Turn left for $\frac{1}{3}$-mile ($\frac{1}{2}$-km) and then right at a public footpath sign through a gate and along a track. Bear left with the track and pass a gate in the field corner on the right.*

5 *About 150 yards (135 metres) past the gate, cross the fence on the right (no stile) and head to the left-hand corner of the nearest hedge. Cross over the fence (again no stile) and walk along the left-hand edge of the field to the stile in the corner.*

3 *Go down the steps, over the stile, and follow the path to the road. Turn left as far as The Lynmore public house.*

2 *Take the right-hand path uphill towards the trees on top of the earthworks and walk through the wood, eventually rejoining the path at the edge of the hill by the gravel steps.*

Moat

Sharpenhoe

Priory Farm

Settlement

NT

(A)

NT

Swithcombe Hill

A 6(T)

Sharpenhoe Road

Masts

Streatley

6 *Take the path ahead uphill through the wood. Go up the steps and turn left along the distinct path, eventually emerging from the wood into a field.*

7 *Walk to the right of the hedge ahead and into the next field. Turn left along the edge of the field to the road and turn left back to the car park.*

1 *Start from the National Trust car park beside the Sharpenhoe-to-Streatley road. From the access road, head half-left down a grassy path just beyond the car park fence and go through the wood, bearing right uphill at the fence and on up the steps.*

A The name clappers comes from the French word for rabbit warren – *clapier*, for it was the Normans who introduced the rabbit into Britain.

The earthworks comprise an artificial mound constructed for the rabbits to dig their burrows, and were very common in medieval times. It was unused by the end of the medieval period, however, and planted with beech trees in the 1840s.

An excavation in 1979 revealed that there was also some sort of Iron Age occupation of the site.

IVINGHOE BEACON

6 miles (9½ km) Moderate/Strenuous; muddy in sections

This walk incorporates one of the best viewpoints in the Chilterns which, although not the highest, is certainly one of the most extensive, with views on all points of the compass. It lies at one end of the official Ridgeway path and is understandably one of the most popular spots on the escarpment.

2 Take the second gravel track on the right and follow the grassy path between the wooden posts just to the right of a private drive. Go straight on over a stile down to the Ridgeway Path above Incombe Hole, and turn left downhill to a fence.

1 From the B489 at the foot of the Beacon, take the road to Ringshall and follow the signs to the car park just off the road. Walk back to the road and turn left.

3 Do not cross the stile but turn left along the fence to another stile and enter the wood.

4 Go straight ahead where the paths cross and then right at a T-junction.

5 Take the path just to the right of the cottage and enter the wood. After about 200 yards (180 m), turn left up a path by a large beech tree, and go straight ahead to a T-junction 20 yards (15 m) short of the road. Turn right for about 75 yards (70 m) then cut left to the road by the public footpath sign. Turn right.

6 Turn left up the drive to Ward's Hurst Farm. At the farmyard, turn left and then right down a dirt track, continuing downhill on a path by the left-hand edge of the field. Continue to the right of the trees, over a barbed-wire fence to the bottom of the field.

Map labels: B 489, Wireless Station, Masts, Gallows Hill, 230, Ivinghoe, Tumulus, Beacon Hill, Ivinghoe Hills, Dagnall, B 4506, A 4146, Pitstone Green, Windmill, NT, Incombe Hole, The Coombe, Ringshall Coppice, NT, 249, The Ridgeway, Ivinghoe Common, Ringshall, NT, Aldbury, T

Over

20

11 *Turn left downslope to the left of a small hill down to the road. Turn left on the verge path back to the car park.*

10 *Go through the hedge into the next field and bear half-left to the top of Gallows Hill (this path may be under crops). Go half-left across a track, walk through a field and follow a grassy path to the summit of the Beacon.*

9 *At the T-junction, turn right along the edge of the field and then left at the corner.*

8 *Turn left at a public bridleway sign and walk around the perimeter of the radio installation.*

7 *Cross the stile and turn left along the edge of the field to a drive. Turn right and then left at the road.*

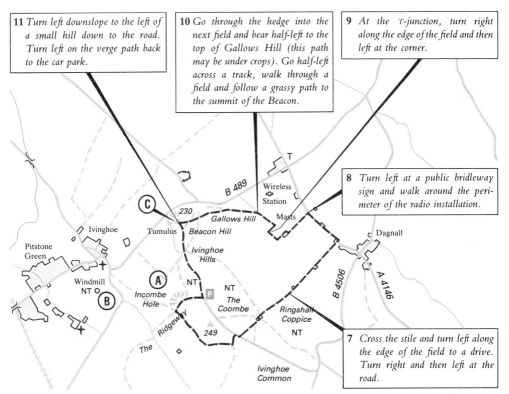

A Incombe Hole is 250 feet (76 m) deep and a superb example of the dry valleys – or coombes – that are a characteristic of chalk country.

B Pitstone Mill stands in the middle of a field and looks curiously isolated. It is one of the oldest post mills in Britain and dates from around 1627. It was working until damaged by a freak storm in 1902 and given to the National Trust in 1937. Restoration did not begin until 1963, however, but now the mill is in fine condition

and contains several interesting features, including the tailpole and wheel and the conventional ladder entrance.

C At a little over 750 feet (228 m), this bare hill gives superb views in all directions. One of the most prominent features to the north is the church at Edlesborough, standing apart from the village on what could be an artificial mound. Just beyond it is the large sixteenth-century barn of Church Farm. To the east is the white lion

denoting the proximity of Whipsnade Zoo. The scene to the southwest presents a good view back down the escarpment.

The site was inhabited by people of the Iron Age, and there are traces of ancient fortifications thought to be one of the earliest Iron Age forts in the country, dated at around 600 BC. The hill was also a burial ground, as evidenced by the presence of two bowl barrows, and it would, of course, have made a superb site for a beacon.

EAST GINGE AND SCUTCHAMER KNOB

6¾ miles (10¾ km) Moderate/Strenuous; muddy in parts

This is a superb walk among some of the best downland scenery. The route climbs the scarp slope from which there are wide, airy views, and then moves away from the ridge among rolling countryside and along intimate, enclosed valleys. Do not expect to have the scenery to yourself, though, for, as well as other walkers, this stretch of the downs is popular with horse riders.

A This viewpoint overlooks the Thames valley to the Chilterns. Between are two of Oxfordshire's most prominent landmarks – the twin, tree-topped hills of Wittenham Clumps and the cooling towers of Didcot power station. At a height of 375 feet (114 m) and with a base diameter of 300 feet (91 m) they would be difficult to conceal and, indeed, seem to reappear from every piece of high ground in several surrounding counties.

The power station covers an area of 370 acres (150 ha), and was built on the former site of the Army's Central Ordnance Depot. Its construction cost £100 million and it first became operational in 1970. The four 500 megawatt generating turbines are fuelled by coal, brought by rail from the East Midlands coalfields, and produce enough power for ten cities the size of Oxford.

Water for cooling is pumped from the Thames at a rate of 45 million gallons (205 million litres) a day. The towers were split into two groups of three spaced ½ mile (800 m) apart in an attempt to minimize their impact on the environment. In height, however, they are dwarfed by the 654-foot (199 m) chimney.

Light can have an interesting effect on the towers, making them appear larger or smaller according to conditions and, during heat haze or mist, they can appear from a distance to float off the ground.

The huge complex of buildings in the foreground is the Atomic Energy Research Establishment at Harwell. It was founded in 1946, with the original task of researching into all aspects of atomic energy. Today, however, its work covers a wide range of scientific disciplines, much of it sponsored by industry. It employs around 4000 personnel, making it one of the largest contract research organizations in the world.

B Scutchamer Knob is a Saxon burial mound that once stood about 77 feet (23 m) high before suffering severe damage by nineteenth-century archeologists. Its unusual name probably originates from *Cwicchelmshlaew* – the burial place or 'law' of Cwicchelm, a West Saxon king who died in around AD 600. The place has been of some importance in more recent history when a moot was held here once a month to deal with local crime and taxes. It was also the site of a large fair associated with East Hendred.

Over

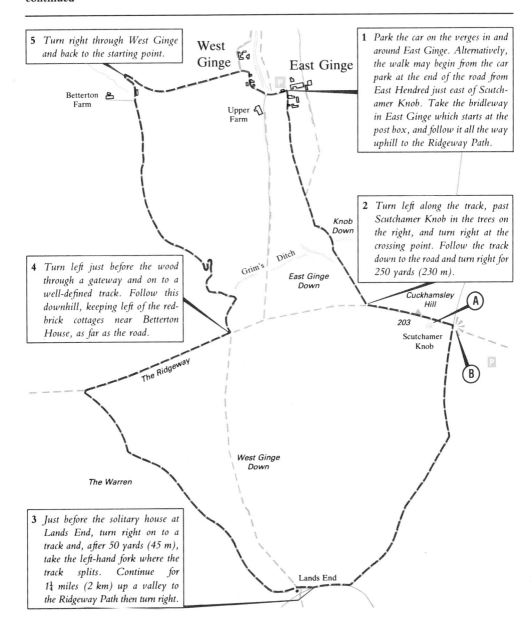

5 *Turn right through West Ginge and back to the starting point.*

West Ginge

East Ginge

1 *Park the car on the verges in and around East Ginge. Alternatively, the walk may begin from the car park at the end of the road from East Hendred just east of Scutchamer Knob. Take the bridleway in East Ginge which starts at the post box, and follow it all the way uphill to the Ridgeway Path.*

Betterton Farm

Upper Farm

2 *Turn left along the track, past Scutchamer Knob in the trees on the right, and turn right at the crossing point. Follow the track down to the road and turn right for 250 yards (230 m).*

Knob Down

Grim's Ditch

East Ginge Down

4 *Turn left just before the wood through a gateway and on to a well-defined track. Follow this downhill, keeping left of the red-brick cottages near Betterton House, as far as the road.*

Cuckhamsley Hill

A

203

Scutchamer Knob

B

The Ridgeway

West Ginge Down

The Warren

3 *Just before the solitary house at Lands End, turn right on to a track and, after 50 yards (45 m), take the left-hand fork where the track splits. Continue for 1¼ miles (2 km) up a valley to the Ridgeway Path then turn right.*

Lands End

MINSTER LOVELL AND CRAWLEY

3½ miles (5½ km) Easy; a little mud

This is a pleasant stroll through gentle, pastoral scenery, and ideal for a lazy summer's day or an evening's perambulation. Here to the north-west, the influence of the Cotswolds is apparent, not only in the buildings and walls, but also in the tranquillity of the Windrush valley.

The ruins, meadow, and river form a harmonious group – almost as if they had been artistically arranged by some medieval landscape designer.

A Half of the name of Minster Lovell derives from the presence of a small priory, first recorded in the twelfth century but later dissolved in 1487. The other half is the name of the family who held the land from Norman times until 1487. The present church is largely fifteenth century and, together with the manor house, is largely attributable to William Lovell.

His grandson, Francis, was a Yorkist, known as 'Lovell the Dog' in a Lancastrian rhyme, who disappeared after the Battle of Bosworth in 1485. He fled to the Low Countries and returned two years later with the pretender Lambert Simnel in an attempt to dethrone Henry VII. The scheme ended in defeat at the Battle of Stoke, and Lovell was last seen escaping over the River Trent. Tradition has it that he reached his family home and hid in a secret chamber known only to one trusted servant. Unfortunately, the servant died and Lovell starved to death.

But the story does not necessarily end there for, in 1708, a secret chamber was found in the house. Contained within it was the skeleton of a man seated at a table – just possibly the remains of Francis Lovell.

Over

3 Cross the stile and follow the left-hand field boundaries, eventually passing through a gate on to a track.

4 Turn right to the road and then right again along the main road across the river.

5 Turn left through a gate 50 yards (45 m) from the bridge and follow the path through the fields to another gate. Pass through, and turn right over a stile to the road.

2 After the last house, cross the stile in the hedge on the right and take the footpath signposted 'To Crawley', crossing the meadow in the direction of the distant mill chimney.

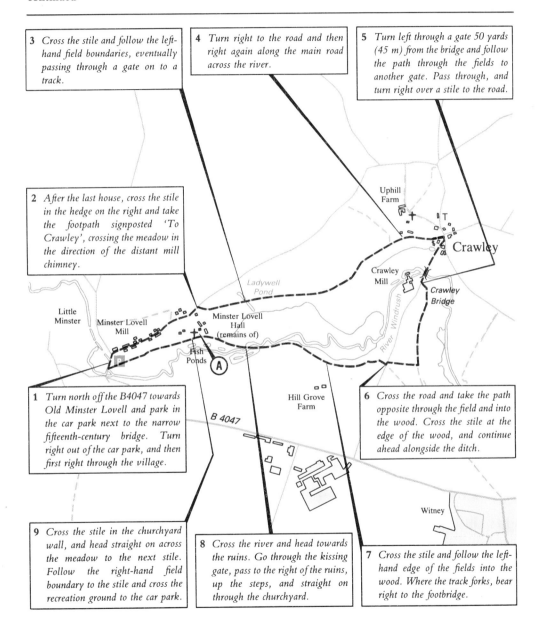

1 Turn north off the B4047 towards Old Minster Lovell and park in the car park next to the narrow fifteenth-century bridge. Turn right out of the car park, and then first right through the village.

6 Cross the road and take the path opposite through the field and into the wood. Cross the stile at the edge of the wood, and continue ahead alongside the ditch.

9 Cross the stile in the churchyard wall, and head straight on across the meadow to the next stile. Follow the right-hand field boundary to the stile and cross the recreation ground to the car park.

8 Cross the river and head towards the ruins. Go through the kissing gate, pass to the right of the ruins, up the steps, and straight on through the churchyard.

7 Cross the stile and follow the left-hand edge of the fields into the wood. Where the track forks, bear right to the footbridge.

ALDBURY AND THE BRIDGEWATER MONUMENT
2¼ miles (3½ km) Easy; one climb, some mud

Aldbury is an outstanding Chilterns village with many of the elements of a 'typical' English scene – the green, old cottages, pond, and church. Despite the nearby rail connection to London, it has resisted the architectural impositions of the commuter belt.

The walk continues along an ancient hollow way up to Aldbury Common, now National Trust property. The Monument appears suddenly in a clearing and, if energy permits, provides a superb viewpoint.

1 *Park in the village by the pond. Walk up Toms Hill Road for 100 yards (90 m); then turn left along the public bridleway. Follow this uphill through the wood, continuing straight on along the main track up to the monument.*

2 *Turn right on to the road leaving the monument and after about ¼ mile (400 m) turn right on to a short section of tarmac road which soon becomes a dirt track through the woods. Follow this straight on, ignoring all other paths until it crosses another track next to a small pond (in the trees ahead left).*

Pitstone Common

B

Tumulus

Bridgewater Monument

Thunderdell Cottages

Aldbury Common

Aldbury

A

NT

4 *Turn right and follow the path down through the wood until it meets a wide track. Turn left and retrace the route back to the village.*

Gryme's Dell

3 *Turn right and go past a cottage on the right, to where the path forks by a waymarked post. Ignore this and continue on for 20 yards (18 m) to a second post.*

A The village name derives from the Saxon *Aldeberie*, meaning 'old fortified place', although the site of the fortifications is unknown. Life in the village was centred on farming but, in the nineteenth century, many villagers made straw plait, encouraged by the straw hat industry around Luton. The Victorian stocks and whipping post have been restored. The pond used to be deeper and provided water for the farm animals. Some of the houses date from the 1600s but most are eighteenth or nineteenth century – former farmhouses and tradesmen's dwellings restored for modern habitation.

B The Bridgewater Monument was erected in 1832 to commemorate the third Duke of Bridgewater, a pioneer of the canal age. It is 108 feet (33 m) high, but the climb to the balcony is rewarded by fine views of the surrounding countryside.

26

Walk 12
GREAT COXWELL GREAT BARN AND BADBURY HILL
5¾ miles (9¼ km) Moderate; some mud after rain

The Great Barn can come as a surprise to the first-time visitor because its size and location are concealed until one is close upon it. It is described as one of the finest surviving medieval barns in England.

The walk continues through attractive farmland, and those in need of rest and refreshment can stop at the pub in Coleshill. The encampment at Badbury Hill has a commanding position between the Vale of White Horse and the

Thames Valley. It is a moderate ascent to the top but the views and beautiful woodland provide a relaxing end to the walk.

9 *Cross this stile and aim for the next one approximately 100 yards (90 m) from the near corner of the field. Aim for the farm buildings. Cross the stile and turn right down the track.*

10 *Walk through the double gates ahead and across the field, following the hedge on the left.*

11 *At the corner of the field, cross the ditch and follow the field boundary into the wood. Follow the path through the wood to the top of the hill. Bear left around the wood to the car park.*

8 *At the road junction, go straight ahead through the gap into the field. The path may be indistinct but follows the left-hand hedge all the way to Fern Copse. Go straight ahead over stiles and a footbridge, and follow the hedge boundary on the left.*

1 *The walk starts and finishes at Badbury Hill car park. Turn left on to the road and, after 500 yards (455 m), right to Great Coxwell.*

Brimstone Farm
Coxwell Wood
Fern Copse
Badbury Hill   156
Colleymore Farm
B 4019   Great Coxwell
Faringdon
Great Barn NT
Coleshill
Flamborough Wood
Ashen Copse Farm

2 *Turn right into Puddleduck lane; stay on the track through fields.*

7 *Walk straight ahead through the gates and turn right on to the main road opposite the church. Turn left at the Radnor Arms.*

3 *Turn left at the junction of the tracks.*

6 *At the corner of Flamborough Wood, bear right across the field and pass just to the left of a clump of trees. Cross the stiles ahead and aim for the white gates just to the right of the distant tower.*

4 *Immediately after the house on the left, turn right through the gate and follow an indistinct path straight ahead, keeping close to the field boundary. Pass into the next field through a gap in the hedge and to the right of farm buildings.*

5 *Cross the main track and continue on a well-defined track.*

A Great Coxwell Great Barn is an outstanding barn built by the Cistercian Order in the thirteenth century. Much is original, and the supporting timbers for the roof are particularly interesting. Information inside.

B Viewpoint of Downs to the south-east. On a clear day, it is possible to pick out the ancient chalk figure of the White Horse.

C No-one has dated these ancient earthworks at Badbury Hill for certain but they are possibly Neolithic. Originally, there were two banks and a ditch but only traces now remain. There are good views over the Thames Valley and pleasant woodland.

BOARS HILL

3¼ miles (5¼ km) Easy; some mud after rain

Boars Hill lies 3 miles (5 km) south-west of Oxford above the drone of the city's incessant traffic. From its 540-foot (165-m) summit, gentle pastoral slopes dip towards the Thames and give relatively unobstructed views of the 'Dreaming Spires'.

The Victorian poet, Matthew Arnold, is closely connected with this area and he described the wooded slopes as these 'warm, green muffled Cumnor Hills'.

The woodland grows on an acid soil derived from a capping of sandy rocks and gives shelter to the exclusive houses that line the hillside. In the 1920s, however, the hill was in danger of unwelcome development. This was averted by the Oxford Preservation Trust who intervened by purchasing selected sites on the hill top.

A Jarn Mound occupies one of these sites. It was constructed under the direction of Sir Arthur Evans, the famous archeologist. Work began in 1929 but was wrecked by massive landslips occurring during heavy storms in 1930 and, after a fresh start, was completed in 1931.

The view extends to the Berkshire Downs, Inkpen Beacon, and the Chilterns. The Wild Garden at the base of the mound was also organized by Sir Arthur with the aim of representing wild plants from all parts of Britain.

B This is the spot from which Matthew Arnold took inspiration for *The Scholar Gipsy* and *Thyrsis*. Its value was widely recognized and funds were sent from overseas to the Oxford Preservation Trust to help buy the land and preserve it for posterity.

Over

7 *Take the track on the left, angling sharply back uphill across the field, and enter the wood. Ignore the stile on the right and carry straight on, continuing on the road after leaving the wood.*

6 *Look for the bridleway signs in front of the stone barn and turn left. At the gateway, turn right on to the bridleway.*

Hen Wood

Chilswell Farm

8 *Go past the radio mast, and follow the road round to the right at the farm buildings. Carry straight on at the crossroads down Sandy Lane.*

Youlbury Wood

Chilswell House (Carmelite Priory)

5 *Cross the stile to the right of the farm gates and turn left on the track to the farm.*

9 *Turn left down the narrow path just after the post box, and straight on at the crossing of paths down a slight bank.*

4 *Cross the stile and follow the faint path downslope aiming just to the right of the farm buildings.*

Jarn Mound

P

A

10 *Turn left at the junction of paths, and then right just in front of the stile to walk through the trees.*

Old Boars Hill

B

3 *Turn left, and then almost immediately right by the post box in the wall (not down the driveway). Follow the path through the wood and along the right-hand edge of the field.*

Foxcombe Hill

Wooton

Boars Hill

11 *At a sharp right turn, turn left through the kissing gate and walk up Matthew Arnold's Field to the gate in the corner.*

1 *Park in the lane by Matthew Arnold's Field. Walk the few yards back to the T-junction, and take the path off to the left. Go through the gate, and climb the steps to Jarn Mound (these are very uneven and steep).*

2 *From the viewpoint, retrace the path back to the road. Turn right, then right again in front of Matthew Arnold's Field on to the footpath and continue as far as the road.*

SEVENBARROWS

4½ miles (7¼ km) Easy/Moderate; muddy in parts

There are few navigational demands on this walk for the tracks are wide and clearly visible. The Downs are, of course, an important centre for racehorse training, as evidenced by the numerous gallops laid out on the turf. The local industry is said to have had its beginnings in the early eighteenth century at the regular race meetings held by the Earls of Craven, who created nearby Ashdown Park.

The misnamed Sevenbarrows is a remarkable group of Bronze Age tombs built by the Beaker people. These continental immigrants used the Ridgeway initially as one of their routes into the centre of England, and have left traces of their culture alongside or nearby many sections of the ancient track.

Even older than the Beaker tombs is a chambered long barrow lying just to the north and built by their Neolithic predecessors – a visible testimony to the historic significance of this site.

A There are certainly more than seven barrows. In fact, it is thought there were originally more than forty in all – many having disappeared under the plough. About twenty can still be traced, most of them of the bell-shaped design used on male graves. There are, however, some of the disc-and-saucer-shaped barrows used in the burial of women.

Over

0   1 mile

0   1 km

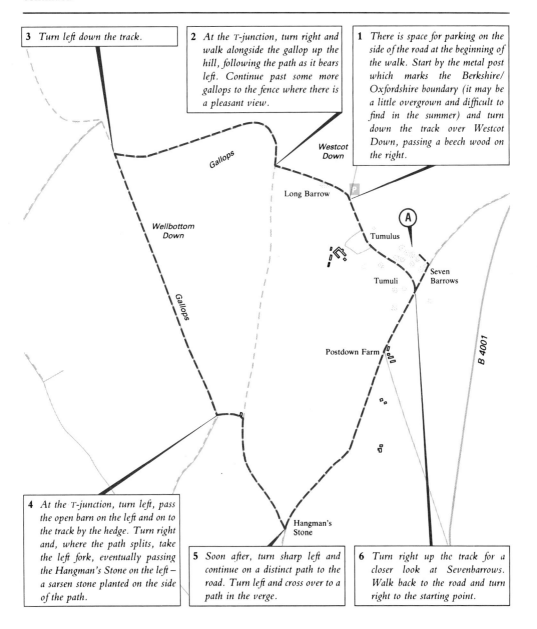

3 *Turn left down the track.*

2 *At the T-junction, turn right and walk alongside the gallop up the hill, following the path as it bears left. Continue past some more gallops to the fence where there is a pleasant view.*

1 *There is space for parking on the side of the road at the beginning of the walk. Start by the metal post which marks the Berkshire/Oxfordshire boundary (it may be a little overgrown and difficult to find in the summer) and turn down the track over Westcot Down, passing a beech wood on the right.*

Gallops

Westcot
Down

Long Barrow

Wellbottom
Down

Gallops

Tumulus

(A)

Seven
Barrows

Tumuli

Postdown Farm

B 4001

4 *At the T-junction, turn left, pass the open barn on the left and on to the track by the hedge. Turn right and, where the path splits, take the left fork, eventually passing the Hangman's Stone on the left – a sarsen stone planted on the side of the path.*

Hangman's
Stone

5 *Soon after, turn sharp left and continue on a distinct path to the road. Turn left and cross over to a path in the verge.*

6 *Turn right up the track for a closer look at Sevenbarrows. Walk back to the road and turn right to the starting point.*

31

SUTTON COURTENAY/ABINGDON

5 miles (8 km) Easy

This route never strays far from the Thames. It gives a particularly good vantage point of Abingdon, a town which grew up around its seventh-century abbey. The river played an important part in the town's prosperity and, by the time of the Dissolution in the fifteenth century, Abingdon Abbey was the sixth richest in the country.

Since 1974 Abingdon has been part of Oxfordshire but, for many years, it was the county town of Berkshire. From 1930 to 1980 it was the sole manufacturing base for MG cars.

A The village takes its name from one Reginald de Curtenai, to whom it was granted in 1161. It is a large village centering on its tree-lined green and full of varied and noteworthy buildings one of which – the twelfth-century Norman Hall – is one of the oldest inhabited houses in Berkshire.

Near the Fish Inn stood a mill which was notorious for charging the heaviest toll on the river. In an unusual arrangement, the river ran under the floor of the mill which meant that the miller opened the weir at his own inconvenience and expense – hence the excessive charge. The problem was resolved by the construction of Culham Cut in 1809 after which the mill fell out of use. The cut also had the benefit of creating a beautiful backwater at Sutton Pools. Here the river falls some 8 feet ($2\frac{1}{2}$ m) into the lasher pool, creating a constant cascade of foaming white water.

B The beautiful stone bridge was built in the fifteenth century by the Brotherhood of the Holy Cross, a guild of Abingdon merchants, as part of an overall scheme to improve communications into and out of the town. It was superseded by the present bridge in 1928.

It spans the Swift Ditch, the original course of the Thames until the tenth and eleventh centuries when the monks of Abingdon Abbey dug the channel that now flows through the town. By the early 1600s, however, there were problems with shallows and shoals and it was decided that Swift Ditch would henceforth be the main channel.

Consequently, one of the first pound locks on the Thames was built here in the 1630s. It was then in use until 1790, when the merchants of Abingdon, anxious to divert trade back to the town, decided to build Abingdon lock on the old channel. Swift Ditch was abandoned and is now only navigable by canoe but the lock remains and was so strongly built that, but for a new pair of gates, could still be used today.

C This is one of the best views of Abingdon, with the graceful seventeenth-century spire of St Helen's rising above eighteenth-century almshouses.

The iron bridge nearby marks the point where the Ock flows into the Thames. It was erected in 1824 as a monument to the Wiltshire and Berkshire canal which opened in 1810 and joined the river a little further down. It ran from near Trowbridge, to Swindon and along the Vale of White Horse to Abingdon, carrying mainly coal, grain, and Bath stone, but ceased to operate in 1906.

D The Causeway, together with Abingdon bridge and Culham bridge, were built from 1466–22 by the Brotherhood of the Holy Cross to improve communications and provide a dry route in times of flood. At the time, the town competed with Wallingford but these improvements attracted the main road west out of London, which now passed through Abingdon instead of the older crossing of Wallingford.

Over

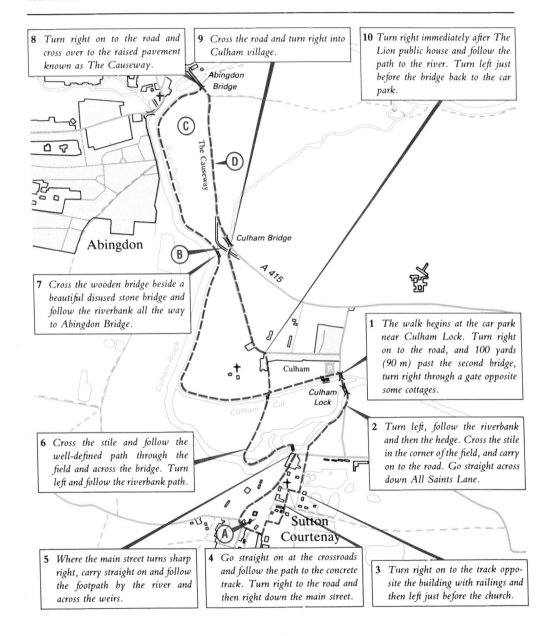

8 *Turn right on to the road and cross over to the raised pavement known as The Causeway.*

9 *Cross the road and turn right into Culham village.*

10 *Turn right immediately after The Lion public house and follow the path to the river. Turn left just before the bridge back to the car park.*

Abingdon Bridge

The Causeway

Abingdon

Culham Bridge

A 415

7 *Cross the wooden bridge beside a beautiful disused stone bridge and follow the riverbank all the way to Abingdon Bridge.*

1 *The walk begins at the car park near Culham Lock. Turn right on to the road, and 100 yards (90 m) past the second bridge, turn right through a gate opposite some cottages.*

Culham

Culham Lock

Culham Cut

Culham Reach

6 *Cross the stile and follow the well-defined path through the field and across the bridge. Turn left and follow the riverbank path.*

2 *Turn left, follow the riverbank and then the hedge. Cross the stile in the corner of the field, and carry on to the road. Go straight across down All Saints Lane.*

Sutton Courtenay

5 *Where the main street turns sharp right, carry straight on and follow the footpath by the river and across the weirs.*

4 *Go straight on at the crossroads and follow the path to the concrete track. Turn right to the road and then right down the main street.*

3 *Turn right on to the track opposite the building with railings and then left just before the church.*

33

COOKHAM AND CLIVEDEN REACH

5½ miles (8¾ km) Easy

Here on the lower reaches, it seems that the river is always busy. Nevertheless, between the superb beech trees of Quarry Wood and the imposing view of Cliveden House there lies what many believe to be the river's most beautiful stretch.

2 *Turn left just before Moor Hall on to a footpath running between some buildings, and continue on, crossing a stile where the path bears right.*

1 *Start from the car park just off the B4447 at Cookham Moor. Go towards Cookham and turn sharp right at the memorial cross.*

9 *At the road, turn left, then right again on the A4094, finally turning left down the high street and returning to the car park.*

3 *Cross the stile and carry on over the farm track along the right-hand edge of the field.*

8 *Turn left through the woodland where the path ends. Keep on this path (ignoring the road on the right) to a stile at the end of the wood. Take the path ahead as indicated.*

4 *At the field boundary, turn right over the first footbridge, then left at the second and cross the field. Where the path meets a track, carry straight on.*

Cookham

Moor Hall

Cliveden House

NT

A 4094

River Thames

Maidenhead

Boulter's Lock

Slough

6 *Cross the bridge and continue straight on over a stile into a grassy field. Turn left and keep close to the hedge, turning left again over a stile about 50 yards (45 m) past the entrance to the garden centre. Follow the path across the fields, and go straight ahead at the road.*

5 *At the gate, turn right and follow the footpath across the field. Turn left alongside the ditch and continue over a track (the path may be overgrown in parts) as far as a wooden footbridge.*

7 *Take the footpath opposite the road junction; then turn left and follow the road down to Boulter's Lock. Turn left and shortly branch off to the right along the riverside path.*

A This is one of the best-known locks and, in Edwardian days, was a very fashionable social centre. The Inn was built in 1726 and converted from a flour mill – 'boulter' is another name for a miller. It is the longest and deepest lock – 200 feet (60 m) long and falling nearly 8 feet (2½ m).

B The first house was built in 1666 but the present one dates from 1851. It was bought by the American William Waldorf Astor in 1893 for six million dollars and, during this century, became renowned for its social scene and political scandal.

C Cookham's fine buildings include its seventeenth- to eighteenth-century houses, its old pubs (Bel and the Dragon is fifteenth century), and its church. Near the bridge is the boathouse of the Queen's Swanmaster who, every July in an ancient ceremony, 'ups' the young swans and marks their beaks for their owners.

NETHER WINCHENDON AND CUDDINGTON
2¼ miles (3½ km) Easy

This is an undemanding walk across a peaceful stretch of the Thame valley and through two attractive Buckinghamshire villages.

Nether Winchendon is a mellow village of colour-washed cottages clustered around its tiny green. The church was rebuilt in the nineteenth century but the interior was relatively untouched and well worth a visit. One resident of the village was Lettice Knollys, daughter of the Puritan statesman. She became a friend of Elizabeth I and was the mother of the 'Splendid' Earl of Essex.

Cuddington has a cosy feel, full of picturesque cottages gathered around the village greens and lining the narrow lanes. Some of the village walls are composed of 'wichert' – a traditional Buckinghamshire mixture of chalky marl with straw which gives typically soft, rounded shapes.

1 *Park in Nether Winchendon and proceed to the postbox in the centre of the village. Take the minor road opposite the church and walk on past Nether Winchendon House to the mill.*

2 *Turn right in front of the mill, cross a stile, and go on to a footbridge over the Thame. Continue down the left-hand side of the fields and up to another footbridge.*

3 *Turn right beside a wooden fence (and note the fossil ammonite on the left opposite the first cottage) and down a narrow lane to the road. Turn left to the green and then right along Holly Tree Lane.*

6 *Fork left just before the stone bridge, cross over the river once more, and continue on to the road. Turn right back to the starting point.*

5 *Turn right down the concrete road and continue straight on when it becomes a dirt track.*

4 *Bear right down Spurt Street and at the end, continue straight on along the main road for about 50 yards (45 m).*

A Nether Winchendon House has been the home of the Bernard family for over 200 years, one of whom, Sir Francis Bernard, was governor of New Jersey and Massachusetts in 1760. The original medieval and Tudor house received extensive additions from 1790 to 1815.

CHESHAM AND LITTLE MISSENDEN

8½ miles (13½ km) Strenuous; some mud

This is a very good day's walk with some superb Chiltern scenery over wide rolling fields. Part of the route lies between the enclosing walls of a dry valley, along a typical Chiltern 'bottom', and provides an unusual sense of seclusion. Another feature of this walk in dry country are the river valleys, for Chesham lies at the source of the Chess, and Little Missenden stands beside the Misbourne.

Although Chesham is an historic town, there are few old buildings left, but the final part of the route passes some of them by. The town was known for lace, chair leg bodging, and woodware. Along the High Street stood the shop belonging to Arthur Liberty, who traded here before moving his business to Regent Street.

Little Missenden, on the other hand, lies in a secluded valley and has been bypassed by both road and rail. It is a most attractive village and has featured in more than one film. It contains several Georgian houses, including Missenden House built in 1728, but the manor house is mainly Jacobean. The most remarkable building, though, is the church, which celebrated its millenary in 1975. Once through the porch, one has the feeling of stepping back through the centuries.

6 Cross the stile into the wood and follow the path along the right-hand edge of the wood until it merges with a wider path. Turn left and keep on the main path, eventually passing a metal gate on to a small road. Turn right.

5 Turn right down the concrete track to Reddings Farm for 150 yards (135 m), before turning right beside a wooden fence. Continue by the fence, past the farm buildings, and then left to a stile. Go on ahead down the left-hand side of the field to the fence and turn right as far as a stile.

4 Take the second path on the left and follow the track along the valley bottom. It becomes a grassy path then a dirt track once more before reaching the road. Turn left uphill.

3 Just before the fence, bear left down a path to a field. Go half-left down to the road and cross the stile opposite. Follow the path half-left to a stile in the hedge and then walk on along the distinct path to the road. Turn right.

2 Turn right along the rough road in front of the church and continue on along the left-hand edge of the field ahead.

7 Turn left down a narrow path just past 'The Huddle'. Cross the stile, walk along the left-hand edge of the field to the next stile, and then on along the right-hand side of the field to a wooden fence. Cross this and bear slightly left to a stile in the hedge. Turn left along the road for 50 yards (45 m).

1 Park in the car park near the library. Go over the roundabout and walk a short way along the Chartridge road before turning left along a tarmac path through the park, heading towards the church.

South Heath

Redding's Farm

Chesham

B 485

The Hyde

White's Wood

Mantle's Wood

Hyde Heath

Bray's Wood

River Misbourne

Amersham

A 413

(A) Little Missenden

Over

36

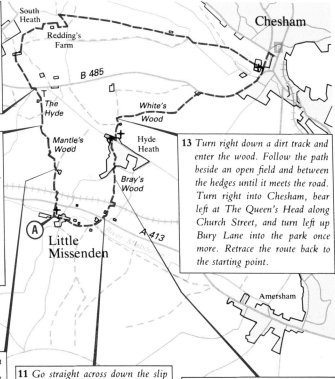

8 *Turn right down the drive to 'The Hyde'. When it turns sharp right, continue on along the path to the left of the holly trees and down to a stile. Cross this and the one ahead, continuing straight ahead over the field to the marked stile in the far corner.*

9 *Cross the stile, go over the track and into the wood ahead on a short path which emerges into a field. Turn right along the edge of the field and, just after a sharp left bend, follow the grassy track that cuts across the field towards the wood ahead. Turn right in front of the wood, eventually bearing left with the path into another wood ahead.*

13 *Turn right down a dirt track and enter the wood. Follow the path beside an open field and between the hedges until it meets the road. Turn right into Chesham, bear left at The Queen's Head along Church Street, and turn left up Bury Lane into the park once more. Retrace the route back to the starting point.*

10 *Where the paths cross before a barn, turn right down to a stile, and then shortly right over the railway bridge into a field. Go straight ahead to the road and take the path opposite along the left-hand edge of the field, over the River Misbourne and on to the road. Turn left through the village back up to the main road.*

11 *Go straight across down the slip road and over the stile on the left. Walk along the left-hand edge of the field to the stile and turn right to the bridge. Cross over the railway and turn left between the fences to a stile at the end. Cross this and walk along the left-hand edge of the field to the wood.*

12 *Follow the path through the wood to the road, and turn right as far as a T-junction by the post office. Turn right for 50 yards (45 m), then left down the signposted footpath, continuing past the last house on the right for 100 yards (90 m).*

A The church has an Anglo-Saxon core but some of the building materials are much older – parts of the church, including the chancel arch are built of Roman brick.

The arcades are Norman but the most notable feature is probably the 10-foot (3-m) high figure of St Christopher, painted in the thirteenth century but not discovered until the 1930s. To the right is more thirteenth-century work on a series of panels depicting the life of St Catherine.

There is much more of interest to see inside, and the church guide is most informative and easy to follow.

Walk 19
MARLOW
4 miles (6½ km) Easy

Marlow is a lively, attractive town and a popular place of residence since the eighteenth century. The pinnacled church tower and the elegant white suspension bridge are probably the first features to attract the eye, although both of these are Victorian and so not particularly old. Near the bridge is the Compleat Angler, a famous hotel renamed after Izaak Walton's book, published in 1653. Its garden contains a large willow said to have been planted by the Duke of Wellington.

The rest of the town abounds in fine buildings and is well worth the extra time to look around.

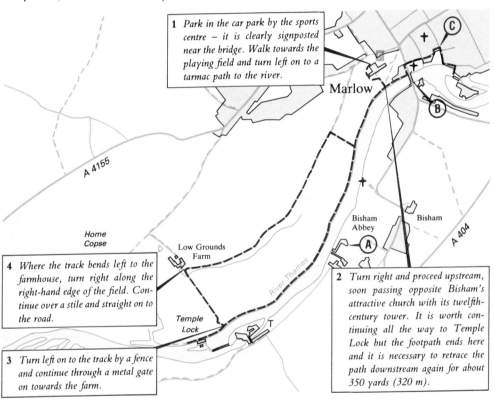

1 *Park in the car park by the sports centre – it is clearly signposted near the bridge. Walk towards the playing field and turn left on to a tarmac path to the river.*

Marlow

A 4155

Home Copse

Low Grounds Farm

Bisham Abbey

Bisham

A 404

River Thames

4 *Where the track bends left to the farmhouse, turn right along the right-hand edge of the field. Continue over a stile and straight on to the road.*

Temple Lock

2 *Turn right and proceed upstream, soon passing opposite Bisham's attractive church with its twelfth-century tower. It is worth continuing all the way to Temple Lock but the footpath ends here and it is necessary to retrace the path downstream again for about 350 yards (320 m).*

3 *Turn left on to the track by a fence and continue through a metal gate on towards the farm.*

A Bisham Abbey was founded in the twelfth century but the present house is mainly Tudor, built for Henry VIII for his fourth wife, Anne of Cleves. Up to 1768, it belonged to the Hoby family and, for three years, they were custodians of the Princess Elizabeth, who stayed here during Mary's reign.

It is reputedly haunted by the ghost of a Lady Hoby, who beat her slow-witted son to death for making a mess of his copybooks.

Interestingly, some blotted sixteenth-century copybooks were found during renovation work some years ago. Now the Abbey is owned by the Sports Council who organize coaching for a wide range of physical activities.

Over

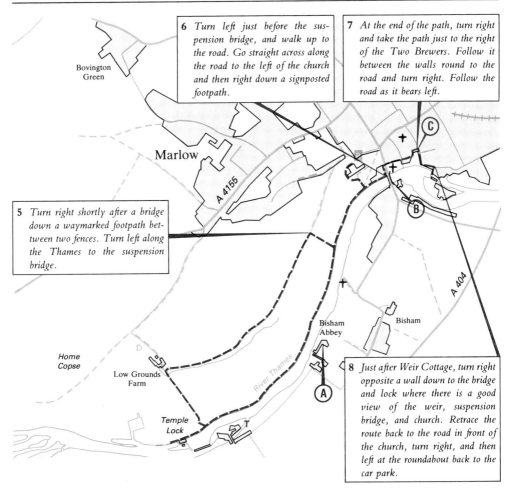

6 *Turn left just before the sus-pension bridge, and walk up to the road. Go straight across along the road to the left of the church and then right down a signposted footpath.*

7 *At the end of the path, turn right and take the path just to the right of the Two Brewers. Follow it between the walls round to the road and turn right. Follow the road as it bears left.*

5 *Turn right shortly after a bridge down a waymarked footpath bet-ween two fences. Turn left along the Thames to the suspension bridge.*

8 *Just after Weir Cottage, turn right opposite a wall down to the bridge and lock where there is a good view of the weir, suspension bridge, and church. Retrace the route back to the road in front of the church, turn right, and then left at the roundabout back to the car park.*

B There has been a bridge here for at least 600 years, but the present structure dates from the 1830s. It has a span of 225 feet (68 m), and its designer was William Tierney Clark. Marlow bridge is one of the few reminders of his work, for his two other bridges of note – at Hammersmith and Budapest – were either re-placed or destroyed in war.

C Bargemen would bring their horses along this somewhat con-torted route when they wished to proceed along the river between the lock and the bridge. There was, as now, no towpath on this section and, as the distance between the two points is about ¼ mile (400 m), it necessitated the use of a very long piece of rope!

BECKLEY AND OTMOOR

5 miles (8 km) Moderate; muddy – wellingtons are useful after rain

This flat, solitary countryside has been called the loneliest place in Oxfordshire. It is frequently water-logged, not that this bothered the Romans who routed part of the Alchester to Silchester road straight over the moor. Now another road is planned – the latest in a series of events that have threatened to alter the character of the place. All have aroused strong opposition – first the enclosures, then the reservoir, and now the M40. The land is certainly worth conserving for it is home to rare woodland butter-flies, a wide range of wetland plants, and many birds.

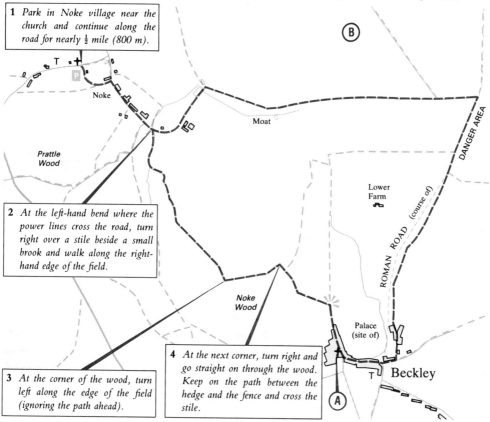

1 *Park in Noke village near the church and continue along the road for nearly ½ mile (800 m).*

2 *At the left-hand bend where the power lines cross the road, turn right over a stile beside a small brook and walk along the right-hand edge of the field.*

3 *At the corner of the wood, turn left along the edge of the field (ignoring the path ahead).*

4 *At the next corner, turn right and go straight on through the wood. Keep on the path between the hedge and the fence and cross the stile.*

A The main feature of this attractive village is its church, still mainly composed of its original fourteenth- and fifteenth-century stonework. Some of the features inside include thirteenth-century wall paintings and a thirteenth-century stone font and chest.

The village is also the setting of the novel *Cripps the Carrier*, written by R D Blackmore, author of *Lorna Doone*.

B The two small gorges near Islip and Oddington have ponded the waters of the River Ray,

Over

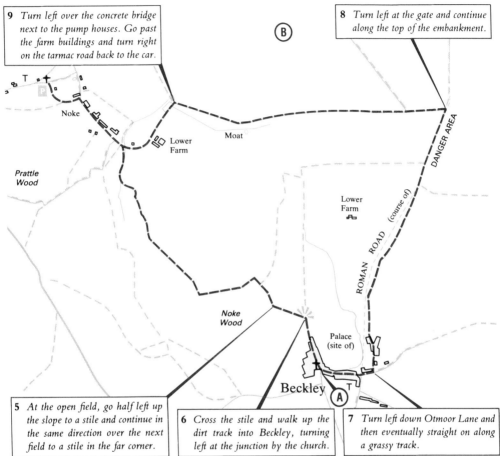

9 *Turn left over the concrete bridge next to the pump houses. Go past the farm buildings and turn right on the tarmac road back to the car.*

8 *Turn left at the gate and continue along the top of the embankment.*

Noke

Moat

Lower
Farm

Prattle
Wood

Lower
Farm

ROMAN ROAD (course of)

DANGER AREA

Noke
Wood

Palace
(site of)

Beckley (A)

5 *At the open field, go half left up the slope to a stile and continue in the same direction over the next field to a stile in the far corner.*

6 *Cross the stile and walk up the dirt track into Beckley, turning left at the junction by the church.*

7 *Turn left down Otmoor Lane and then eventually straight on along a grassy track.*

causing it to spread its alluvium laterally over the adjacent land. Otmoor is surrounded by its 'seven towns', which sit on islands of drier ground.

For centuries these villages enjoyed several rights of common but these were threatened by an enclosure award of 1829. Violence erupted and gangs of men tore down bridges, gates, and fences. Eventually troops and police were drafted in to restore law and order. Nevertheless, it was 1835 before the rioters finally gave up the struggle.

In 1966 the Water Resources Board saw the moor as a potential site for a reservoir which would have covered 4000 acres (1600 ha) if the plan had not been scrapped.

In 1981, however, the government published its proposal to extend the M40 over Otmoor to the West Midlands. In the considerable outcry that followed, the first two routes directly over the moor were abandoned and now the preferred route skirts just to the east.

Walk 21
CHEQUERS AND COOMBE HILL
5½ miles (9 km) Moderate; some mud

This is the Chilterns countryside at its best and the scenery is complete – superb escarpment views, magnificent woods, attractive downland, an ancient trackway, and an imposing historical mansion. The landscape is generously draped with dense green canopies which, in the autumn, make a wonderful wall of colour.

Chequers nestles in the folds of the land and lends a dignified air to the scene. But, throughout the route, most walkers are probably anticipating the quality of the view that awaits them at the end of the walk. Generally, there is little disappointment.

A Chequers was built in 1565 but has since been considerably enlarged and altered. It has passed through the hands of several families – the Hawtreys, the Crokes, the Russells, and then this century to Lord Lee of Fareham, who gave it to the nation in 1917 to be used by Prime Ministers as their country retreat. David Lloyd George was the first to use it but it was particularly popular with Sir Winston Churchill during the war. It was he who ordered the planting of beech trees along the main Victory Drive.

B In 1918, Lord Lee also donated the site of Coombe Hill, now owned by the National Trust. It is a very popular spot and, at 842 feet (257 m) forms the highest viewpoint in the Chilterns. It is not, however, the highest point – this occurs a few miles to the north-east in Wendover Woods.

The monument commemorates the Boer War and is a well-known landmark for many miles around. It has been struck by lightning several times and, in 1938, one strike virtually reduced it to rubble. The place is also a Site of Special Scientific Interest (SSSI) and, with two soil types, there is an interesting comparison between the birch, heather, and gorse vegetation on the clay-with-flints and the juniper-clad chalk slopes.

Over

42

0 _____ 1 mile

0 _____ 1 km

1 Park on the verge close to the footpath or, alternatively, in the car park next to the crossroads at Butler's Cross ½ mile (800 m) away. Take the well-defined path up and across the field then turn right down the track to the road.

2 Turn left along the road for 25 yards (23 m) then left over a stile. Follow a faint footpath up the hill, over a stile, and along the side of Beacon Hill where there is a good view of some splendid woodland. Enter the wood.

3 Cross the field into the next wood.

4 Cross the stile and walk along the edge of Whorley Wood. Cross the next stile and follow the edge of Maple Wood.

5 Cross the stile and, after 75 yards (70 m), turn left down the Ridge-way Path. Cross Chequers drive and continue on to the road.

6 Take the path into the wood on the opposite side of the road. Follow it uphill, continuing straight on where the paths cross.

7 At the T-junction, turn half-right and follow the path to the stables.

8 At the stables, cross the stile ahead, then walk diagonally left uphill across the paddocks, crossing several stiles to the road.

9 Turn right on to the road and then first left. Pass The Fox public house, and take the tarmac path straight ahead. At the fork, take the bridleway to the right.

10 Take the left-hand path over the stile and continue to the left of the iron fence until the path is diverted to the left.

11 Where the paths meet, cross the stile opposite and walk along the left-hand edge of the field. At the corner of the wood, head for the monument and viewpoint, eventually taking the path down the spur of the hill.

12 Just before the road, turn sharp left and take the lower right-hand path along the edge of the wood to where the paths cross. Turn right to the road then right again to the starting point.

Elllesborough

Coombe

B 4010

257

Beacon Hill

Coombe Hill

NT

Whorley Wood

Chequers

A

B

Maple Wood

Ridgeway

Buckmoorend

Dunsmore

Princes Risborough

43

BRILL AND MUSWELL HILL

5 miles (8 km) Moderate; one steep climb – muddy in parts

Brill has been named twice – by the Britons as *bre* 'hill' and then by the Saxons as *hyll*. The site commands wide views over Otmoor and beyond to the Cotswolds while Muswell Hill affords excellent views to the north and east.

8 *Turn right, noting Boarstall Tower on the left, and walk through the village to the road junction. Turn left.*

9 *Turn right at the public bridleway sign, and walk up the left-hand edge of the field to the gate in the corner. Continue on uphill beside the hedge as far as the road.*

10 *Turn right and then left at the signpost on to the track. Soon after bearing right, look for a sign marked* PRIVATE *and follow the direction arrow to a stile in the fence on the right. Continue straight on following the step in field level to the road. Turn left back to Brill Common.*

7 *Cross the stile and footbridge, across some uncultivated ground to a stile, then angle half-right across the field towards the church as far as the road.*

1 *Park the car on Brill Common. Starting from the windmill, turn right down the tarmac road in front of The Pheasant, and walk for a short distance along South Hills, taking the track on the right where the road forks.*

6 *Turn left and almost immediately left again over a stile. Follow the path over a footbridge, through a plantation to another stile in a fence. Cross this and walk along the right-hand edge of the field to the far corner.*

2 *Turn right at a waymarked stile just after the last house, and follow the left-hand edge of the field. After about 100 yards (90 m) cross over the ramshackle gate into the neighbouring field and turn right towards the middle of the bottom fence.*

5 *Turn left over a stile just after the house, and walk along the left-hand edge of the field for about 150 yards (135 m). Turn right at the waymarked post and head towards the distant farm buildings. Cross over the stile in the next hedge and aim for the gate in the top left-hand corner of the field.*

3 *Walk on the same heading across the next field, cross the stream, and bear slightly left to the fencing in the corner of the field (ignore the gate). Cross over and follow the path to the road. Turn left.*

4 *At the sharp bend, turn left on to Span Green – once a drover's road – and follow the track to the road. Turn right.*

A There have been windmills here since the thirteenth century and the present one, built in 1688, was in use until 1916. The top was pivoted by the tail pole.

Clay quarrying has pock-marked the common. The production of pots, tiles, and bricks was important until the nineteenth century.

B Boarstall Tower was the gate-house to a fortified medieval house which was despoiled in 1646. It dates from the fourteenth-century but has seventeenth-century additions.

STONOR PARK AND TURVILLE

5¾ miles (9¼ km) Moderate/Strenuous; one steep climb

This route contains beautiful park and woodland, passing by one of the foremost stately homes of the area and through one of the prettiest Chiltern villages.

1 Park in the small parking area in Turville Heath just to the east of the triangular road junction. Turn right on to the road for 150 yards (135 m) to a public footpath sign on the left.

2 Turn left down the drive of Saviours, pass to the left of the main gate, and walk ahead to a stile in a fence. Follow the faint path ahead to the next stile; then across the field, skirting the corner of the copse to a gate in the fence.

3 Turn right along the track and continue down the right-hand edge of the fields to a stile in the corner of the copse.

4 Go straight on down to a track and turn left to the road. Turn right past the farm and then left at the T-junction, eventually passing the entrance to Stonor Park.

5 Turn left through the kissing gate at the end of the iron railings and follow the waymarked grassy path uphill and through the park to an iron gate in a fence. Carry straight on into the wood and turn right at a junction with a track. At the next junction, continue straight on to the road and turn left.

6 Turn right down the track opposite The Drover, past the farm, and then straight on across the field to a stile in the fence. Follow the track down to the road and take the path opposite through the field.

7 Go straight on at the field boundary to the road and turn left through the village at the T-junction by the church.

8 Turn left at the public bridleway sign just outside the village and follow the track uphill. Where it bears right, continue ahead over a stile into the wood. Turn right on the track and then immediately left uphill, following the waymarks to another track. Turn right.

9 Turn left at the junction and continue to the road. Bear right and go straight on at the T-junction back to the car park.

Map labels: Ibstone, Turville Heath, B 480, Turville, Windmill, B, Fingest, Turville Court, Balham's Wood, Southend, Great Wood, Whitepool Farm, Stonor House, A, Stonor, Stonor Park (Deer Park)

A Stonor has been a family home for over 800 years. The medieval Catholic chapel has been in continuous use and the house was sanctuary for Edmund Campion in 1581.

B Many of Turville's buildings are sixteenth to eighteenth century. The smock mill above the village was converted to a dwelling in 1973.

CHIPPERFIELD COMMON AND CHENIES BOTTOM

8¼ miles (13¼ km) Strenuous; one climb, some mud

The drama of the Chilterns scarp-land gives way to a progressively gentler landscape to the east. By the time the outskirts of London are reached, the gradients are kinder and the once-dry valleys now contain burbling streams. The Chess is one of these, a small river famous for its trout, winding calmly through its attractive wooded valley.

The river links the two villages of Latimer and Chenies which together were originally called Isenhampstead. Latimer received its present name from the family who were granted the land by Edward III and, today, largely consists of part-timbered and brick cottages peacefully clustered around the small, triangular green.

A The Pond of the Twelve Apostles is a tranquil spot set deep in the wood of Chipperfield Common. It was surrounded by twelve lime trees (the Apostles) until one of them – Judas Iscariot – blew down. Nearby is a Spanish chestnut tree with a girth of 21 feet (6½ m) and said to be 300 years old.

B The small green in Latimer contains the covered village pump and a war memorial – nothing too surprising there. What does seem a little bizarre is the third item denoting the burial place of a horse. It was ridden by a French officer who saved the life of Lord Chesham during the Boer War. The officer was killed and Lord Chesham brought the horse back to England where it was eventually interred on Latimer's green.

Over

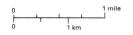

9 Turn right and, where the road turns sharp right, continue straight on along the path signposted Belsize ¾ through the wood. Continue on the main path to an open field; then go straight on to the road.

10 Turn left to a junction and then right uphill back to the car park.

1 Park on Chipperfield Common near The Windmill. Walk across the grass in the direction of the footpath signs, enter the wood, and follow the grassy path on to a dirt path. Continue ahead to the Pond of the Twelve Apostles and skirt round it to the path along the southern edge of the wood. Continue as far as a stile on the left just before a house.

8 Turn right and quickly left over a stile, bearing left on a grassy path by the farm buildings and continuing on at the junction of paths to the road.

7 Turn left, go past the church and, at the left-hand bend, go straight on along the narrow path to the road. Turn left for 100 yards (90 m) and then right over a stile and along the path to the road. Turn right to a T-junction.

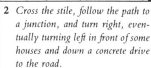

2 Cross the stile, follow the path to a junction, and turn right, eventually turning left in front of some houses and down a concrete drive to the road.

6 Turn left on to a path before the farm buildings and, where it bears right, continue straight on over a stile, along the edge of the field to the road. Carry straight on up to a T-junction.

4 Turn half-right in front of the gates, and on along the path between the trees. Continue past the farm, down the concrete track, and turn right over the stile just before the river. Follow the waymarked path to the road, turn left, and then right through the farm, continuing on the waymarked path along Chenies Bottom to the road.

3 Go ahead up Poles Hill to a junction and turn right. Take the footpath on the left signposted to Chenies and Church End and, at the farm, carry straight on after skirting around the fenced area, continuing through the wood and down to a field and two gates.

5 Turn right, go through Latimer, and eventually turn right through a gate at the public footpath sign. Follow the track to a wooden barrier, take the right-hand path to the next barrier and turn left along a track, over a crossing of tracks, and on towards the farm.

WHITE HORSE HILL AND ASHBURY
7¾ miles (12½ km) Strenuous; two climbs, some mud

This is a vigorous day's exercise that samples both the exposed heights and the peaceful villages of the Vale of White Horse. It is probably the best-known section of the Ridgeway which here is clearly defined between flanking hedgerows. It threads its way past a series of ancient monuments that are shrouded with myth and legend, and it would be a rare visitor who was not even momentarily affected by the mystery and age of it all.

There is often a bracing wind on Uffington Castle – at 855 feet (260 m) that is not too surprising — but the view is worth any effort or discomfort. To the west are the tower blocks of Swindon, further round to the north are the mounds and scarp of the Corallian ridge, while to the east are the inescapable outlines of Didcot Power Station – no view of Oxfordshire would be complete without it! In the Vale below lies a string of villages sited near to the spring line at the junction of the clay and the Greensand bench that runs along the foot of the scarp.

Compton Beauchamp has a beautiful chalk church, and Woolstone is full of attractive thatched cottages but really they are all worthy of further exploration.

A The White Horse still remains a mysterious figure. All that is known for certain are its dimensions: 360 feet (110 m) long and 160 feet (48 m) high. There are several theories regarding its origin. One explains it as commemorating Alfred's victory over the Danes at the Battle of Ashdown in 870. The one given most credence though is that the horse was the tribal symbol to the Dobunni, who occupied the site around the first century AD. The theory is lent weight by the discovery of a Dobunni coin stamped with the figure of a horse. Interestingly, this design has been traced by some experts to the coins used during the reign of Philip II of Macedon, and it is possible that the Berkshire horse may have Greek origins.

Another mystery is how the artist managed to proportion the beautiful flowing lines when the figure can only be seen as a whole from the Vale below. One theory is that Dragon Hill, which may be artificial, served as a vantage point for directing the cutting.

B Tradition has it that it was upon this strange, flat-topped hill that St George killed the dragon, and the bare patches are where the creature's blood spilled to the ground. Yet another legend claims it to be the burial place of Uther Pendragon – the father of King Arthur.

C Uffington Castle is an Iron Age hillfort and possibly related to the White Horse. It encloses 8½ acres (3½ ha) and has a single entrance on the west. Its steep bank and ditch were probably originally strengthened by timber and sarsens.

Much later it became the site of an important fair held every seven years associated with the scouring of the Horse. One regular event was a chase after cheeses that were rolled down the steep coombe nearby known as the Manger. The last fair was held in 1857.

D Wayland's Smithy is an unusual Neolithic long barrow consisting of one burial chamber placed on top of another. Excavations have revealed skeletons and it is probable that it was intended to house the dead of a dynasty. It was constructed in around 2800 BC, the mound composed of material dug from ditches either side and contained by sarsens.

Its name post-dates it by several thousand years, for the Saxons associated the place with one of their gods – Wayland – who forged swords and armour of special powers. It seems he was also a blacksmith since you had but to leave your horse and a coin by the tomb, it is said, to find it miraculously shod on your return.

Over

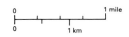

9 Turn left for 50 yards (45 m) and then right over a stile, following the right-hand field boundary to the farm. Cross the stile to the left of the gates and on up to the road. Turn right at the White Horse and continue straight on over the crossroads uphill back to the car park.

1 Park in the car park on Woolstone Hill. Walk up the steps, through the gate, and head half-right towards a distinct track on the distant hill.

2 Cross the road and follow this track uphill; then turn left by the thorn trees to the White Horse. Eventually, retrace the route back to the thorn trees and turn left, past Uffington Castle, and over a stile on to the Ridgeway Path.

8 Turn first left down to Knighton, and carry on through the village. Turn right over a stile by the village sign, over a footbridge and along the path to the left of the trees. Follow the path over more footbridges and stiles, through a small plantation to a raised track.

7 Cross the field to a set of white marker posts, and continue along the waymarked route to the church at Compton Beauchamp. Go through the wicket gate in front of the church and turn left on to the tarmac road, past the pond to the road. Turn right.

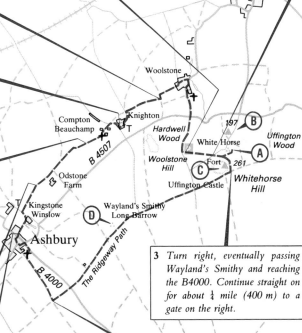

3 Turn right, eventually passing Wayland's Smithy and reaching the B4000. Continue straight on for about ¼ mile (400 m) to a gate on the right.

6 Cross the stile and head across the field to the next stile, through a gate, and on ahead to the left of the farm. Cross the concrete track; go over the stile ahead, and on along to the left of the barbed-wire fence. Continue, following the right-hand field boundaries to a gateway in the corner of the field by Windmillhill Copse.

5 Take the tarmac path opposite, next to the small church, past the pond and up to the road. Cross the road, go ahead up to the way-marked gates, and turn right beside the fence.

4 Turn right through the gate along the edge of the field, and follow the path downhill to a T-junction. Turn right to the B4000 and then left into Ashbury. Turn first left, and follow the road round through the village back to the main road.

BLENHEIM

3¾ miles (6 km) Moderate

0 ⊢————⊤————⊤————⊤————⊤————⊤————⊤————⊤————⊤ 1 mile
0 ⊢————————————————⊤———————————————— 1 km

Blenheim is one of the greatest stately homes in the country, set in 2000 acres (800 ha) of splendid parkland. Queen Anne gave Woodstock Manor and £240,000 on behalf of a 'grateful nation' for Marlborough's victory over the French at Blenheim in 1704. It was built from 1705–22 and designed by Vanbrugh, the grounds later recreated by Capability Brown.

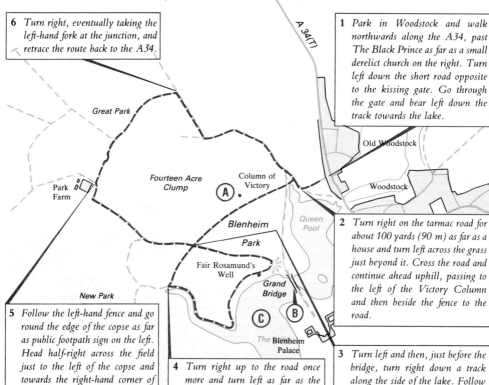

6 *Turn right, eventually taking the left-hand fork at the junction, and retrace the route back to the A34.*

1 *Park in Woodstock and walk northwards along the A34, past The Black Prince as far as a small derelict church on the right. Turn left down the short road opposite to the kissing gate. Go through the gate and bear left down the track towards the lake.*

2 *Turn right on the tarmac road for about 100 yards (90 m) as far as a house and turn left across the grass just beyond it. Cross the road and continue ahead uphill, passing to the left of the Victory Column and then beside the fence to the road.*

3 *Turn left and then, just before the bridge, turn right down a track along the side of the lake. Follow this pleasant track to the western end of the lake and a junction of tracks.*

4 *Turn right up to the road once more and turn left as far as the farm. Turn right in front of the buildings, and cross the stile on the right where the track bends.*

5 *Follow the left-hand fence and go round the edge of the copse as far as public footpath sign on the left. Head half-right across the field just to the left of the copse and towards the right-hand corner of the field. Pass under the barbed wire (no stile here) and on ahead to the road.*

A The Column of Victory was completed in 1730, some eight years after Marlborough's death. The lead statue at the top depicts the Duke in Roman dress and raises the height of the Column to 134 feet (41 m).

B The Duchess quarrelled bitterly with Vanbrugh over the cost of the bridge. It is almost 400 feet (122 m) long but its visible height was considerably reduced when the creation of the lake flooded its lower sections.

C Probably the most magnificent private lake in the country, it was created by Brown in 1764 by damming the River Glyme ¾ mile (1¼ km) west of the bridge.

WATLINGTON HILL

2½ miles (4 km) Easy

Watlington Hill is owned by the National Trust and, at over 700 feet (213 m) high, presents one of the best viewpoints from the Chilterns, overlooking the Oxfordshire plain. A single-line railway used to run along the top of the ridge to Watlington but now there are broad grassy paths brightly coloured with wild basil, marjoram, rock roses, eyebright, and a host of other typical chalk-loving plants.

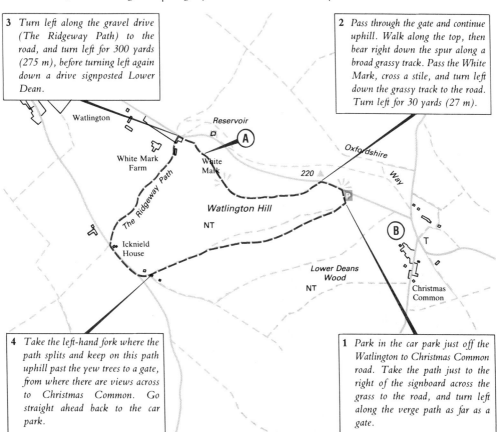

3 *Turn left along the gravel drive (The Ridgeway Path) to the road, and turn left for 300 yards (275 m), before turning left again down a drive signposted Lower Dean.*

2 *Pass through the gate and continue uphill. Walk along the top, then bear right down the spur along a broad grassy track. Pass the White Mark, cross a stile, and turn left down the grassy track to the road. Turn left for 30 yards (27 m).*

4 *Take the left-hand fork where the path splits and keep on this path uphill past the yew trees to a gate, from where there are views across to Christmas Common. Go straight ahead back to the car park.*

1 *Park in the car park just off the Watlington to Christmas Common road. Take the path just to the right of the signboard across the grass to the road, and turn left along the verge path as far as a gate.*

A The White Mark was cut in 1764 on the whim of a Watlington resident who wished to see the village church with a spire. From his window, the church was outlined against the hill and he had the triangle cut where it seemingly joined the top of the church.

B Christmas Common is said to be named from an incident in the Civil War at a time when the Royalists held the higher ground and the Roundheads were centred on Watlington. They declared an unofficial truce and celebrated Christmas Day on the common in 1643.

Walk 28

WEST WYCOMBE AND BRADENHAM

$4\frac{1}{4}$ miles ($6\frac{3}{4}$ km) Moderate; two climbs

This walk contains a mixture of interesting natural and artificial features. The yews at the beginning of the route are an unexpected variation in an area dominated by beech trees, their sombre dark green contrasting strongly with the lighter beech woods that occur later on.

On the historical side, it is an area dominated by eighteenth- and nineteenth-century characters, with the Dashwoods featuring prominently in West Wycombe and the Disraelis settling in or around Bradenham.

West Wycombe is an outstanding village bought in 1929 from the Dashwood family by the Royal Society of Arts, who then handed it to the National Trust in 1934. Its main street is lined with a seemingly unbroken series of picturesque buildings, the most notable being the Church Loft. Here, travellers on their way between Oxford and London would take their rest as guests of the church.

The eighteenth-century house and park are exceptional and largely the work of Sir Francis Dashwood, one of the founder members of the infamous Hell Fire Club which met from time to time in the nearby caves. These were excavated for material to build a new road to High Wycombe, one of Sir Francis's schemes that also provided work for the unemployed after a series of bad harvests. The caves are open to the public.

A The church stands almost 600 feet (182 m) high within the confines of an Iron Age fort that once encompassed 3 acres ($1\frac{1}{4}$ ha) within a rampart and ditch. Sir Francis considerably altered the church, both inside and out, reflecting his peculiar and somewhat eccentric taste. In 1751 he raised the fourteenth-century tower and supplanted it with a golden ball, a well-known landmark for miles around. It can hold about six people and commands superb views over the surrounding countryside, although it was more important to Sir Francis and his associates as a refuge for private drinking parties.

The design of the hexagonal mausoleum was derived from Constantine's Arch in Rome and was built from a bequest of £500 from Lord Melcombe Regis in 1765.

B The manor house is the most imposing building of the village and was the last home of Isaac Disraeli, father of Benjamin who became one of Queen Victoria's prime ministers. Benjamin was thirteen when he arrived at the house and brings it into his book *Endymion*. He eventually bought Hughendon Manor, just a few miles to the south-east. The house was originally Tudor but was rebuilt in the 1670s and, like the village, is in the keeping of the National Trust.

Over

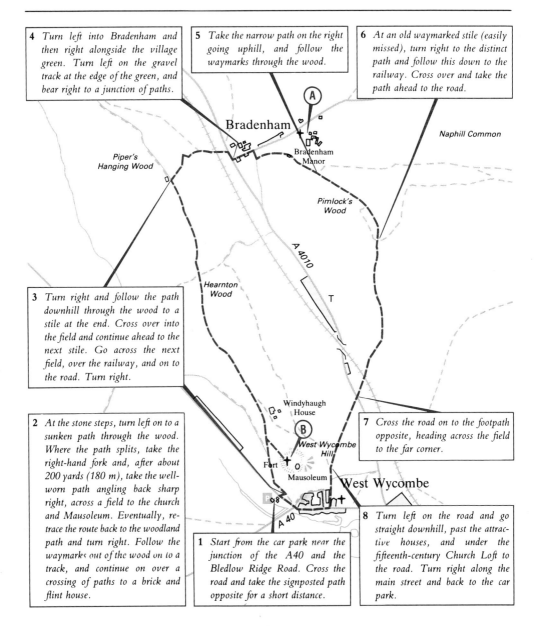

4 *Turn left into Bradenham and then right alongside the village green. Turn left on the gravel track at the edge of the green, and bear right to a junction of paths.*

5 *Take the narrow path on the right going uphill, and follow the waymarks through the wood.*

6 *At an old waymarked stile (easily missed), turn right to the distinct path and follow this down to the railway. Cross over and take the path ahead to the road.*

Bradenham

Naphill Common

Piper's
Hanging Wood

Bradenham
Manor

Pimlock's
Wood

A 4010

Hearnton
Wood

T

3 *Turn right and follow the path downhill through the wood to a stile at the end. Cross over into the field and continue ahead to the next stile. Go across the next field, over the railway, and on to the road. Turn right.*

Windyhaugh
House

7 *Cross the road on to the footpath opposite, heading across the field to the far corner.*

2 *At the stone steps, turn left on to a sunken path through the wood. Where the path splits, take the right-hand fork and, after about 200 yards (180 m), take the well-worn path angling back sharp right, across a field to the church and Mausoleum. Eventually, re-trace the route back to the woodland path and turn right. Follow the waymarks out of the wood on to a track, and continue on over a crossing of paths to a brick and flint house.*

West Wycombe
Hill

Fort

Mausoleum

West Wycombe

A 40

1 *Start from the car park near the junction of the A40 and the Bledlow Ridge Road. Cross the road and take the signposted path opposite for a short distance.*

8 *Turn left on the road and go straight downhill, past the attractive houses, and under the fifteenth-century Church Loft to the road. Turn right along the main street and back to the car park.*

GORING
7¾ miles (12½ km) Strenuous; muddy in parts

Goring is the meeting place of three ancient routes – the Thames, the Ridgeway, and the Icknield Way, and has been one of the most important fords on the Thames since prehistoric times.

Goring and Streatley are twin river towns, one in Oxfordshire and the other in Berkshire, but there was no bridge here until 1838. Before this the river was either forded or crossed by ferry. It was not a particularly safe crossing either and, in 1674, sixty people were drowned when their boat capsized over the weir.

Goring grew very rapidly in Edwardian times and many buildings date from this period. The church, however, dates from the twelfth century and contains a bell that had been in continuous use for 600 years before being placed in its present position in 1929.

2 *Turn right down Whitehills Green Road, bearing left with the road to a roundabout. Turn right and then continue along the tarmac path between the shrubs to a stile. Cross this and walk half-left across the field to the far left-hand corner.*

3 *Turn left along the left-hand edge of the field, cross the stile, and on along the left-hand edge of the next field. At the fence, turn right downslope to a stile.*

4 *Cross the stile and follow the path ahead to the wood, following the main path all the way to a crossing of tracks. Go straight ahead and bear right at a wooden gate, uphill to a T-junction.*

1 *Park in the free car park as signposted from the bridge over the Thames. Return to the main road, turn right, and go over the railway to the T-junction. Turn right, then first left on the B4526 at the Queen's Arms public house.*

5 *Turn left as far as a field gate, then bear left across the field to another gate in the left-hand hedge. Go through on to the road and turn right for 300 yards (275 m) to a T-junction. Turn right and continue down to a road.*

6 *Take the signposted footpath opposite and, where the path splits, take the left-hand fork. Cross a stile on the left just before the farmhouse and walk around the buildings on the right to a stile in the right-hand hedge.*

7 *Cross the stile, walk on to the clearly marked stile in the fence ahead, and continue on the same heading towards the wood.*

Streatley
Goring
Common Wood
Great Chalk Wood
Stapnall's Farm
Gatehampton Farm
Woodcote
B 4526
River Thames
A 329
Coombe End Farm (NT)
Lower Basildon
Hartslock Wood
Basildon House
Coombe Park
B 471
Park Wood
Whitchurch

Over

54

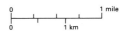

The mill was built in the 1920s, a replica of an older timber building. The lock was first constructed in 1788 and is one of a few that have an extra third pair of gates inside the lock chamber. These effectively make the lock smaller and so save water but they are rarely used.

13 *Turn right on the towpath and then right just before the bridge up to the road. Turn right opposite the Miller of Mansfield back to the car park.*

8 *Cross the stile and go straight ahead, ignoring the minor paths either side, to the gate at the end of the wood. Aim for the left-hand corner of the buildings opposite and go through the kissing gate, over the concrete track, and through the gate opposite. Follow the track all the way to the B471.*

Streatley

Goring   B 4526

Great Chalk Wood

Common Wood

Stapnall's Farm

Gatehampton Farm

Coombe End Farm (NT)

A 329

Lower Basildon

Hartslock Wood

Whitchurch Hill

12 *Go through the kissing gate opposite and, after 100 yards (90 m), turn left down a gravel track. Branch off to the right along a narrow path signposted to Jordleys, and continue down to the river.*

Basildon House

Coombe Park

B 471

Park Wood

Whitchurch

River Thames

11 *Turn left at the public footpath sign down the left-hand edge of the field to the road. Turn right, go under the railway on to a track, and turn right again. Turn left at the junction, and go as far as a crossing of tracks.*

10 *Where the track bears sharp left to Hartslock Farm, go ahead through the wooden gate (ignore the metal one) and continue on the path into the wood, past an attractive view on the right. Follow the waymarks through the wood and on to a path above the Thames, from which there is an unexpected view out over the river. Carry on downhill to a narrow path beside a fence and continue on past Gatehampton Farm on a concrete track.*

Pangbourne

Purley

9 *Turn right, cross the road to the raised pavement, and follow it downhill. At the end of the path, cross the road and turn right down the bridleway signposted to Goring.*

A Until blocked by ice during the Ice Ages, the Thames originally flowed north-eastwards towards the Wash. The river was ponded back and eventually found the easiest route to the sea along the present course. Road and rail routes have made use of the gap.

CHINNOR HILL AND LODGE HILL

7¾ miles (12½ km) Strenuous; several steep climbs

This is an energetic walk that pays ample dividends for the effort involved. The views are wide-ranging and at times – as at Lodge Hill – unexpectedly good.

The walk begins at Bledlow, with its Norman church set in an unusual wooded ravine, and then passes by the village pub which claims to be the only pub in Britain with more than one lion in its title. Nearby is Bledlow Cross, 75 feet (23 m) from side to side and of unknown age, although probably no later than the seventeenth century.

Chinnor Hill stands at around 800 feet (243 m) and, excluding the cement works, offers fine views to the north and west as far as the Cotswolds. Sixty-five acres (26 ha) of the hill were purchased in 1964 by the Berkshire, Buckinghamshire, and Oxfordshire Naturalists' Trust, and contains varied habitats of scrub, wood, and downland.

The route follows the Ridgeway for a short distance where it traverses the isolated scrub-clad pine of Lodge Hill. The views from here are good at any time of year but in spring and summer there is the added bonus of a colourful floral carpet. Among others, there are the purples of wild thyme and basil, the tall yellow spears of the mulleins and the eye-catching white and pink of wild candytuft. It is a relatively quiet part of the long-distance path and offers unobstructed views over the Aylesbury Plain.

A Radnage Church stands curiously isolated from the rest of the village, which is arranged in the typical Buckinghamshire cluster of 'endships'. There were probably two earlier churches here, and the Saxon font, dug up in a nearby field, is thought to be connected with one of them. The square tower, the nave, and the chancel are thirteenth century but were later added to and altered.

Over

0   1 mile

0   1 km

2 Pass to the right of the house ahead and take the left-hand fork going uphill through the wood. Follow the waymarks to the top and to the viewpoint at the clearing, eventually continuing on the path to a track at the end of the wood.

1 Park in Bledlow and proceed to the Lions of Bledlow public house. Take the nearby footpath going off across the field until it meets a dirt track. Turn right and go uphill as far as a junction of paths by some houses.

11 Cross the stile and go straight over the track to the stile ahead. Walk along the right-hand edge of the field over more stiles back to the road in Bledlow.

3 Go straight on past the small parking area on to a road. Follow this to a junction and turn left.

10 Cross the stile opposite and follow the left-hand hedge to a stile. Cross this and walk along the right-hand edge of the adjacent field to the stiles on the right. Cross these and head half-left across the field to a stile in the far hedge.

4 Turn right down a signposted footpath beside a partially concealed water tower and continue by the fence on the left, downhill through the wood to another fence.

5 Turn left along the fence and follow the path as far as a T-junction. Turn right on the tarmac road to another Tjunction, and turn left.

9 Pass through a tall hedge, turn immediately left uphill, and cross a stile. Walk along the ridge, with its airy views either side, and then descend following the left-hand field boundary. Turn left over a stile, and then along a distinct path to the road.

6 After 150 yards (135 m), turn left at a public footpath sign, cross the stile, and head down the field to the next stile in the far left-hand corner. The route goes left here but it is worth a small diversion to Radnage church across the road, eventually returning to the road and turning right.

7 Turn right at the second public footpath sign and follow the path up to the road. Go straight across along Routs Green and turn right just before the end of the road. Follow the road round on to a dirt track and through a gate.

8 Follow the left-hand fence; then continue downhill to another gate. Cross the field to the far left-hand corner, and go through into the next field, following the track uphill and around to the right of the scrubland.

Bledlow

T

Chinnor

Upper Icknield Way

Bledlow Cross

Ridgeway

Bledlow Great Wood

Chinnor Hill

Lodge Hill

Woodlands Farm

Manor Farm

Sunley Wood

Rout's Green

Radnage

Crowell Wood

A

WALLINGFORD

6 miles (9½ km) Moderate

Wallingford is an interesting old town in a pleasant riverside setting. The ruined castle site is a peaceful spot which may delay the start of the walk but there is plenty to see later on, including good views to the Chilterns and a stretch of the Thames that shows off the town's attractive waterfront.

A These are the remains of what was once one of the largest castles in the land. There was probably a Roman fort here and the Danes are recorded attacking a Saxon stronghold on the site. William the Conqueror recognized the strategic importance of the river crossing and ordered the construction of a castle, which was completed in 1071. Matilda fled to the castle from Oxford and was besieged by Stephen, this period of national unrest finally being settled by the Treaty of Wallingford in 1153.

The castle played its last historical role during the Civil War when, as a Royalist stronghold, it withstood a sixteen-week siege. Cromwell saw it as a possible future threat and had the castle destroyed in 1652.

B The linear earthwork of Grim's Ditch can be traced for many miles from Wiltshire, across the Berkshire Downs and east of the Thames, into the Chilterns and Buckinghamshire. It would seem to be some sort of a barrier across the ancient routes of the Ridgeway and Icknield Way.

Its origin and purpose are unknown but it seems probable that it was built by pre-Roman tribes. It may have been a tribal boundary, a defensive structure, or a physical limit to grazing livestock.

The name Grim is another word for Woden, the Saxon god. The Saxons may have been as puzzled by the ditch as we are today and attributed the mysterious earthwork to the magical powers of Woden (compare the Wansdyke – Woden's Ditch).

C Wallingford was a fording place in prehistoric times and, for a long time, lay on the main route out of London to the west country. Its importance declined, though, with the opening of Dorchester bridge.

The first documentary evidence of a bridge occurred in 1141, although there was probably one in existence much earlier than that. Today's structure dates from the thirteenth century but has since been considerably altered.

In 1641 the Royalists blew up four of the arches and replaced them with a wooden drawbridge to improve the town's defences. In 1809 the three river arches were widened by several feet on the upstream face and given rounded profiles – those on the downstream side kept their original pointed shape.

It is said that the town once had thirteen or fourteen churches but the Black Death badly decimated the population and only three now remain. St Peter's is certainly the most visible with its unusual eighteenth-century spire dominating the scene from the river.

Wallingford is one of the oldest Royal Boroughs, receiving its charter some thirty-two years before London in 1155. There are many attractive buildings including the town hall dating from 1670, 500-year-old Flint House – now the museum, and the Lamb Arcade, which was once a sixteenth-century inn.

Over

3 Turn right along the towpath and, just before the bridge, bear right back on to Castle Lane. Turn left to the main road; then left over the bridge.

4 Turn right just before the campsite entrance down a track. Where the path splits by a gate, take the left-hand fork between the trees, and continue as far as a concrete track.

5 Turn right then left over a stile. Go half-left to the next stile and then half-right to the far corner of the field. Turn left to the road.

2 Turn right at the cemetery down the waymarked path as far as a stile and track. Cross to the stile ahead and walk on beside the iron fence to a stile by the river.

6 Turn right, then left on the Ridgeway Path along Grim's Ditch, and continue on to the road. Turn right as far as a gate on the right with a footpath sign.

1 Park in the town centre or in the car park by the river on the Crowmarsh Gifford side of Wallingford Bridge. Go to the western end of the bridge and turn down Castle Lane, bearing left in front of the farm and past the castle entrance. Continue on the track between the walls to the road and turn right.

7 Head half-right towards the distant silos, through the gateway in the hedge, and on along the path to the farm. Walk to the left of the silos and straight ahead, bearing left around the farmhouse.

8 About 50 yards (45 m) from the bend, turn right through an opening in the fence and walk along the right-hand edge of the field by the barbed-wire fence to the road.

13 Walk under the bridge, up the stone steps, and turn right to the starting point.

9 Turn right for about 50 yards (45 m), then left through a partly concealed gate, following the right-hand edge of the field through another gate to the road.

10 Turn right, then left at a public footpath sign down to a stile. Cross the next stile on to the driveway, turn left, and go through the wooden gate by the house. Follow the wall to a double row of barbed wire and on to a stile. Continue down the right-hand edge of the field over a gate, and across a stile.

12 At the sharp right-hand bend, take the concrete path to the left of the farmhouse and cross the stile into the field. After about 100 yards (90 m), turn left at the waymarked post across the field to the river and turn right to the bridge.

11 Turn right to the tarmac road and continue on through the college, eventually reaching a paved path. Carry straight on.

COOKHAM DEAN AND WINTER HILL

3½ miles (5½ km) Moderate; two climbs

Cookham Dean is a village spaced out around its common land with a considerable portion owned by the National Trust. It stands above steep beech woods and its undulating site has earned it the nickname of 'miniature Switzerland'.

The open land has gradually been enclosed to provide village amenities. The parish church was begun in 1844, a relief to the vicar of nearby Cookham who complained that the distance between the populace and the parish church at Cookham was too great and encouraged a good deal of Sabbath-breaking. More land was enclosed in 1899 for an infant school but there is still a surprising amount of farmland in the village and the route passes unexpectedly through a fruit-growing area.

Several well-known literary figures are connected with the area. Shelley often walked in Quarry Wood, as did Jerome K Jerome. Kenneth Grahame grew up in Cookham Dean and moved back to the village from London from 1906 to 1910. Thus, he was living here when his best-known work was published in 1908. The inspiration for *Wind in the Willows* came from the bedtime stories told to his son Alistair and beginning on the boy's fourth birthday in 1904. Grahame knew this part of the Thames very well and was probably the background for the adventures of the animal characters. It is thought that Quarry Wood is the real-life counterpart of the fictional 'Wild Wood', which was put into its global context by Rat:

'Beyond the Wild Wood
comes the Wide World.
I've never been there
and I'm never going.'

A Winter Hill is a well-known spot with a renowned view of the river extending from Henley to Maidenhead. The summit lies at around 225 feet (68 m) and the outlook is more semi-industrial than rural. Nevertheless, despite the roads and built-up areas, there is still plenty to catch the eye – boats on the flooded gravel pits and an aerial view of Marlow with its church spire and suspension bridge.

Over

0   1 mile

0   1 km

6 *At the junction, take the path angling back sharp left uphill to a point where several tracks meet, and take the third track from the left going uphill and to the right.*

5 *Take the signposted path through the trees to a gravel drive and turn right. Pass to the right of the gate of Rivendell and on to a path through the wood. Where the path splits, take the right-hand fork and, at the roadside, turn right downhill to the road. Take the footpath opposite and continue through the wood.*

4 *Go straight ahead up Job's Lane to a road and turn right to the viewpoint at Winter Hill. Eventually, retrace the route back to the western end of the first lay-by.*

Marlow

River Thames

Winter Hill

Ⓐ NT

Cookham Dean

A 404

Quarry Wood

NT

NT NT NT

Bisham

Bisham Abbey

Bigfrith Common

3 *Take the signposted path opposite across Bigfrith Common, and continue straight on through the farm to the road. Continue on for 100 yards (90 m); then turn left at the footpath sign to a road.*

The Hockett

Bigfrith

Mount Hill 111

7 *At the next junction, take the right-hand fork up the embankment to where it meets another path near the edge of the wood. Turn left, then immediately right at the marker into the field.*

Cookhamdean Common (NT)

P

Park

Wood

1 *Park in the small unmarked car park on the Pinkneys Green Road at Cookhamdean Common. Head for the far left-hand corner of the field ahead, then follow the track through the trees to a road and turn right to a junction.*

8 *Walk beside the left-hand hedge then through the fields down to a track. Turn left to the road then left back to the car park.*

2 *Follow the gravel track on the green opposite, turning left after 50 yards (45 m) down a track and on to a path leading to the road. Turn right to the crossroads.*

HAMBLEDEN/MEDMENHAM

8 miles (12¾ km) Moderate/Strenuous

This walk contains choice sections of Thames and Chilterns country-side. There are stretches through beautiful woodland, a walk along a lovely part of the Thames, and a visit to one of the most attractive of all Chilterns villages.

The Hambleden valley extends from the Thames to Fingest, about 4 miles (6½ km) away, and is exceptional for its string of un-spoilt villages. Hambleden itself is a National Trust village and is a very restful sort of place to end a long walk.

1 *Leave the car in the village car park. Go through the iron gate, and head diagonally across the field to a kissing gate in the hedge. Take the path opposite, which eventually climbs through a beautiful wood.*

2 *Where the footpath meets a track, look for a stile leading into the corner of a field (this can easily be missed). Enter the field and keep the wood close on the left. At the corner of the wood, cross the field in the direction of the distant buildings, crossing a track and eventually joining the road.*

3 *Turn left and, at the sharp left-hand bend, go straight on and over a stile. Walk ahead across the field and, at the next stile, bear a little to the right into the field. The path may be indistinct but a way-marked stile in the hedge will soon come into view. Cross this stile and turn right on to the road.*

4 *Turn right just after a house called Widefield through a con-cealed gate and along an overgrown path to a stile. Cross this and aim for a stile in the far corner. Cross the track and enter the wood, bearing right almost immediately, and follow the waymarked path through the wood.*

5 *Cross the stile and follow the left-hand edge of the field, crossing stiles and a track into the next wood. Follow the clear path through the wood to a road, turn left, and then right on the A4155.*

Map labels: Marlow, Hambleden, Rotton Row, Heath Wood, Brockmer End Farm, Ridge Wood, North Cot Wood, Widefield, A 4155, ROMAN VILLA (site of), Mill End, Hog Wood, ROMAN VILLA (site of), R.A.F. Station, Aston, Medmenham, A 4155, Fort, Research Institute, River Thames, P, A

A Hambleden has everything expected of an English village – the green, the church, and the old flint and brick cottages forming a unified cluster, with the seven-teenth-century manor house making the scene complete.

The site was occupied in the Iron Age and in Roman times, evidence of which was unearthed during an excavation in 1911 alongside the road to the mill.

More recently, several well-known people have been associated with the village. Thomas de Cantelupe was born here, later Bishop of Hereford and friend of

Over

0   1 mile

0   1 km

11 *Go through the gate by the bridge and turn right, past the Stag and Huntsman to the car park on the right.*

6 *Turn left down the signposted path along the driveway of Abbey Lodge. Cross a small bridge and turn right through an iron gate.*

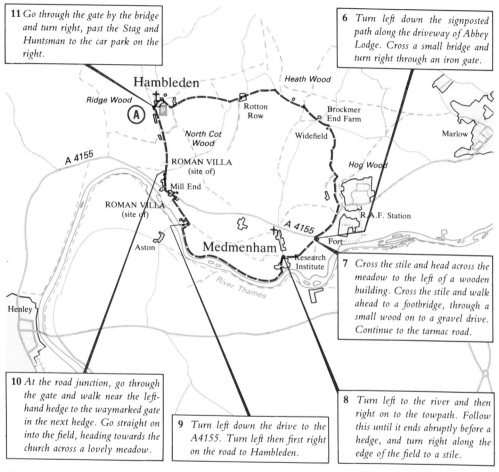

7 *Cross the stile and head across the meadow to the left of a wooden building. Cross the stile and walk ahead to a footbridge, through a small wood on to a gravel drive. Continue to the tarmac road.*

10 *At the road junction, go through the gate and walk near the left-hand hedge to the waymarked gate in the next hedge. Go straight on into the field, heading towards the church across a lovely meadow.*

9 *Turn left down the drive to the A4155. Turn left then first right on the road to Hambleden.*

8 *Turn left to the river and then right on to the towpath. Follow this until it ends abruptly before a hedge, and turn right along the edge of the field to a stile.*

Simon de Montfort and also the last Englishman to be canonized before this century. It is also the birthplace of the Seventh Earl of Cardigan, the same who led the Charge of the Light Brigade. In the churchyard is the grave of the First Viscount Hambleden – W H Smith – founder of the company that bears his name.

The church was begun in Norman times and still has its original font, but there have been alterations and additions in nearly every succeeding century. The spire was rebuilt in 1721 after the original Norman structure collapsed in 1703. In the eighteenth century, the village gained most of the bells from Fingest church when the latter's incumbent lost a wager.

These villages have remained peaceful despite the proximity of the main road. East Hendred is a harmonious blend of timber, brick, tile, and thatch beside a maze of backroads, and is worthy of thorough investigation.

In medieval times Ginge Brook powered fulling mills. It was also used for retting (soaking) flax, and the villages developed a prosperous linen and wool industry. Today, the area is important for racehorse training.

4 *Go through the gate, cross the stile ahead, and continue down the right-hand side of the field. Cross a stile and walk to the two footbridges ahead.*

5 *Cross the footbridges, bear left on to the track and, after 50 yards (45 m), take the path between the fences to the left of the driveway. At the road, turn right to a T-junction.*

6 *Turn right along Cat Street, bear left, and turn right past the cemetery. Go through the gate and continue straight on down the tarmac path to the road. Turn left back to the church.*

A 417

Manor Farm

East Hendred

West Hendred

P

Jesus Chapel

P

The Mill

A

Lydebank Plantation

Goldbury Hill

Park Hill

B

3 *Just after the post office, follow the sign and turn right into a private driveway – an unlikely start to a footpath! Pass through the gate on the left and walk between the two gardens. Cross the stile and follow the right-hand field boundary as far as a thatched cottage.*

2 *Continue straight on, over a stile, and across a small field towards the church. At the road, turn right through the village.*

1 *Park in East Hendred and start the walk at the crossroads near the church. Go uphill along Newbury Road and, after 150 yards (135 m), turn right into Horn Lane. When the road turns sharp right, continue straight on into The Lynch, and over a junction to a crossing track.*

A The church has several items of interest. The faceless clock, dated 1525, may be the oldest working turret clock in the country. It chimes the quarters and hours and, every three hours, strikes out a hymn tune. The unusual thirteenth-century lectern is the oldest of its kind in England.

B Until 1620, a great district fair was held extending all the way from Scutchamer Knob to East Hendred, then important for sheep and wool. It was abolished to encourage the growth of East Ilsley, further south on the Downs.